HUNGARIAN METRICS

RESEARCH CENTER FOR THE LANGUAGE SCIENCES

INDIANA UNIVERSITY

Thomas A. Sebeok *Chairman*

Andrew Vázsonyi *Associate Chairman, Publications*

HUNGARIAN
METRICS:

Some
Linguistic
Aspects
of
Iambic
Verse

Andrew Kerek

Published by
INDIANA UNIVERSITY, BLOOMINGTON
Mouton & Co., The Hague, The Netherlands

INDIANA UNIVERSITY PUBLICATIONS

URALIC AND ALTAIC SERIES

Editor: John R. Krueger

Editor Emeritus: Thomas A. Sebeok

Volume 117

ISBN 87750-163-7

Library of Congress Catalog Card Number: 73-635569

Orders for the U.S.A. and Canada should be placed with Humanities Press, Inc., 303 Park Avenue South, New York, N.Y. 10010. Orders from all other countries should be sent to Mouton & Co., Publishers, The Hague, The Netherlands.

Printed in the United States of America

PREFACE

This book shares the major limitation of all formal approaches to products of literary art. As soon as the whole of a poem is disturbed and the subtle balance of sense, melody, rhythm, and proportion is upset, the poem ceases to fulfill its designed function, for it is no longer capable of reaching what Joseph Conrad called "the secret springs of responsive emotions." By reducing a poem to something less than its inherent totality, formal analysis destroys the calculated poetic effect and obliterates the very identity of the work, inevitably leaving the poet's "ragged hero" on the analytic guillotine beheaded, decimated, lifeless.

Luckily, poems which deserve to survive are immortal; a deserving poem has many existences, and if a few should be victimized the loss is not insufferable. But the gain may be immense: although the metaphoric corpses can no longer give us aesthetic pleasure, they allow us a glimpse into their secret anatomy, and perhaps little by little surrender the well-guarded mysteries of their living counterparts. And should our efforts bring some new understanding, a bit of new insight into the "miracle of language," they were well worth the price; if they should fail, they were worth the try.

I am fully aware that in many ways this study is oversimplified and incomplete, and (perhaps because of their novelty) some of the points are slightly overstated. My purpose was simply to suggest, in an almost programmatic way, what seem to be some fairly plausible reasons for taking another look at 'time-measured' verse in Hungarian, and what, upon further and more careful exploration, might open up new avenues of inquiry into the subject. I was not able to do justice to previous pertinent research, nor was a systematic review of the literature on the subject my aim in this book. References in the notes recognize my indebtedness to many sources. Some particularly relevant and valuable sources, such as Petr Rákos, *Rhythm and Metre in Hungarian Verse* and András Kecskés, *A komplex ritmuselemzés elvi kérdései,* reached me too late to be considered in this book in detail.

I wish to express my thanks to all those who were of assistance while the original version of this study was in preparation (*Stress, Length, and Prominence: Linguistic Aspects of Prosody in Hungarian Quantitative-Iambic Verse,* Ph.D. dissertation, Indiana University, 1968). The comments, criticisms, and encouragement that I received from Professors Thomas A. Sebeok, Robert Wall, and above all Bernard Spolsky, were especially helpful. It goes without saying that for all statements and misstatements in this book I am alone responsible.

Finally, the publication of this book at this time would not have been possible without the generous financial support given by the Faculty Research Committee of Miami University, which I hereby gratefully acknowledge.

February 1971   A. K.
                                                    Miami University (Ohio)

TABLE OF CONTENTS

I
INTRODUCTION

General setting

Since ancient times, students of verse throughout the European literary tradition have been aware of the subtlety and intricacy of metric interplay, and perplexed by the elusive complexity of the interrelationship between metric patterns and the language elements that fill them. The questions that have been pondered for centuries are many: Are the laws that govern the relationship of meter and language basically musical or linguistic? Is the poet free to break rules of his language in striving to meet the requirements set by the metric pattern? Does language or meter have priority in setting the rhythm of verse? Is there an underlying affinity between 'prose rhythm' and 'verse rhythm'? Can metric form and metric function be legitimately divorced in metric analysis? Just as issues like these have been the subject of controversies and disagreements among scholars through the ages, so they continue to be argued today. Although the arguments have taken many forms, they have always involved, implicitly or explicitly, the assumption that an understanding of prosody, of the behavior of language in relation to predefined metric frameworks, is contingent on an understanding of the nature of language in general. Thus a linguistic approach to metrics requires no special justification; verse utilizes language and is therefore a proper subject of linguistic inquiry.[1]

Although there are still many limitations to our knowledge of how language works, and indeed it may be a long time before the present barriers to the mysteries of language are shattered, recent years have witnessed a spectacular progress, a new renaissance in the study of language. By far the most significant aspect of the new trends is an apparent gradual reorientation of the field of linguistics, a redefinition of some of its basic goals in the spirit of modern scientific mentality. The categorization and systematization of observed linguistic facts as ultimate goals of scientific language study have been giving way recently to the desire to explain the facts, to seek out reasons and underlying relationships, and to formulate a theory of language powerful enough to account for the nature of human language ability. By implication, the behavior of language in verse, that is, a speaker's (or poet's) ability to utilize his linguistic resources in specific ways under highly specialized conditions such as metric frames is, in principle, no less 'relevant' or 'interesting' from the point of view of the construction of grammars (i.e. linguistic theories) than linguistic data of any other type. If until recently linguistic theoreticians had tended to disregard forms marked 'literary only' as valid data for grammatical description, it was admittedly due to the purely practical consideration that the inclusion of such forms into the corpus would complicate the task of writing grammars.[2] Because of the many different types, levels, and degrees of variation in the actual use of a language by its speakers, linguists find it necessary to confine the goals of a grammar to the explicit characterization of the linguistic knowledge of a single abstract and idealized speaker. Thus a grammar represents an ideal and never completely realized norm, in terms of which variations may be accounted for; a complete account of a language must in fact specify the relationship of all variations to the grammar.

Literature is of course one typical domain where the occurrence of certain 'stylistically marked' variants of normal ('unmarked') linguistic forms is common, and linguists have not been unaware of the linguistic relevance of literary language as a primary source of important data of this sort. As a matter of fact, much of the discussion of problems of grammaticality and deviance in syntax, which recent interest in the formal characterization of 'linguistic competence' within the framework of the transformational-generative model has produced, directly relates to the language of literary discourse.[3] The discussion has not gone beyond problems of syntax, however; the notion of grammaticality in prosody, and the possibility that poetic language may exhibit cases or patterns of prosodic deviance which can be accounted for by a modification or extension of normal phonological rules of the language, have not been seriously considered. On the contrary, linguistic approaches to metrics tend to stress the fact that the metric principle adopted for a particular verse tradition cannot be at variance with general principles of the language involved, and in fact complete consistency between the meter and language is to be expected.

The latter claim, namely that the abstract extra-linguistic metrical pattern[4] is "perfectly compatible with the linguistic givens of the spoken language,"[5] and therefore, as a rule, is not violated by the poet, deserves closer examination. This hypothesis, recently proposed by Halle and Keyser, is qualitatively different from what at first glance appears to be a weaker version of the same thesis, namely the concept made explicit by linguists of the structuralist school that the organizing principle of a given metric verse form must be a significant (i.e., phonemic) entity in the language involved (such as stress, but not length, in English), since speakers of the language cannot perceive 'sub-phonemic' distinctions.[6] Halle and Keyser apparently understand "linguistic givens" to mean 'linguistic behavior predictable by rules of the grammar,' in the case of English verse those of the English system of stress placement:

> ...A theory of prosody which takes the linguistically determined stresses of a language as part of the elements manipulated by the poet assumes an understanding of what these stresses are. In other words a theory of prosody based, in part at least, upon stress placement necessarily presupposes a theory of stress placement.[7]

The rules of the system of stress assignment, however, which "the prosodist, the poet and the reader, as speakers of the same language, have all internalized," are ultimately tied to other rules of the phonology, to rules of the syntax and the lexicon—to the rest of the grammar; in fact, the hypothesis that all linguistic systems are characterized by a fundamental systematic relationship between syntax and phonology such that syntactic particulars of a sentence determine in part the phonological interpretation assigned to it, is central to the concept of language assumed here. It follows from this concept that the prosodic elements whose alternate presence and absence through the medium of time determines to a large extent the characteristic rhythmic configurations of a language, are assigned to syntactic surface structures and are thus not independent of the rest of the grammar.

Although the Halle-Keyser notion of 'perfect compatibility' between language and meter was originally proposed in connection with the authors' treatment of the Chaucerian tradition of English verse, and eventually may or may not prove to be entirely tenable, it has a certain universal appeal: after all, it is reasonable to suppose that in any language speakers rely on the *same* linguistic knowledge in using their language in verse as in ordinary speech, and if so, both of these facets of language use ought to be subject to essentially the same set of basic principles and explanations. All literature, including the language of versified poetry,[8] is ultimately *sentences,*[9] insofar as the sentence is the basic unit of linguistic expression, although, naturally, literature is a great deal more than just sentences. Thus one might argue that a general condition that any adequate theory of prosody must meet is that it make explicit the relation between the organizing principle(s) of verse and the underlying rhythmic properties and potentials of ordinary sentences in a particular language. If the assumption that such a relation does exist cannot be made, then the theory must explain, and cannot take for granted, the status of 'metric' language with respect to the language as a whole. A case in point is the traditional theory of quantitative prosody in Hungarian.

Purpose of the Study

This study proposes to investigate a segment of Hungarian iambic verse[10] with the aim of formulating a basis for a linguistic characterization of this verse tradition. Such an aim necessitates a new and so far unexplored approach to this verse form. Iambic meter, like all other culturally borrowed metric forms in Hungarian, has been described in the past solely on the basis of the *musical* principle of the alternation of short and long syllables, a principle which is asserted to be inherently independent of accentual conditions in the language (see Chapter II for details). In view of the fact that units of length occur in the sequence of phonemic segments in a metric line as invariant phonological properties (classificatory features) of lexical elements and have not been shown to be a conditioning factor in the assignment of stress, or to bear any significant grammatically definable relationship to other prosodic features of the language, it can be said that the prevalent musical-quantitative view of Hungarian meter is typically non-linguistic.

One important reason why this verse tradition has not been studied on a systematic linguistic basis is no doubt the historically documented[11] fact that Hungarian poets have consciously attempted to adhere to the strictly prescribed basic quantitative rules of Greek-Roman metrics which is known to have had musical origins and to have been generally free from stress.[12] Furthermore, in Hungarian both vowel and consonant length are phonemic, and this has rendered the language particularly suitable for and receptive to the adoption of the classical model with syllable length as its organizing principle. Coupled with the equally well substantiated fact that distinctive stress and strong metric positions (ictus) in this language-specific tradition, unlike in Germanic verse, often do not coincide, the above considerations have imposed a limited range of analysis on the study of Hungarian quantitative meter and have led to the inference that the only valid approach to this verse type is on grounds of the principle of time measurement. This conclusion has remained, if not wholly unchallenged, yet essentially unrefuted so far.

From a linguistic point of view, the musical theory of verse is neither interesting nor satisfactory: it is uninteresting because the metric principle (syllable length) which it assumes is an entity not shown to be related or relatable to the rest of the linguistic system, to the grammar in particular, and hence it can be considered 'linguistic' only in a marginal sense, at best; it is unsatisfactory because it fails to relate the linguistic component of verse rhythm to grammatical and prosodic properties of the sentences that fill the metric framework. Furthermore, by ignoring, and perhaps even disallowing, the paradoxical possibility of treating in terms of *systemic* properties of the poets' *own* language a verse tradition based on a *foreign* model, this theory creates a gap between prosodic characteristics of ordinary discourse and those of metric discourse, a gap which it is inherently unable to bridge. This discrepancy is not adequately resolved, from a linguistic viewpoint, by the implicit traditional assumption that quantitative verse utilizes the natural rhythmic tendencies of the language. The question is, what *linguistic* explanation can be given for these tendencies.

The whole principle of the regular alternation of length units such that long syllables signal rhythmic peaks only by virtue of being long in relation to neighboring short syllables, is untenable even in terms of the metric rules traditionally postulated for Hungarian iambic verse. For, as will be shown in the following chapter, the rules and conventions of quantitative verse that Hungarian poets adopted from other metric traditions had undergone substantial modifications before being generally accepted as a set of norms for iambic verse in Hungarian; specifically, and crucially, the requirement that only long syllables can occupy strong metric positions (ictus) was dropped and *short stressed* syllables came to be accepted as signals of metric prominence, in addition to stressed or unstressed long syllables. The role of stress became significant in other respects as well, to be discussed below; the point to note here is that once the rigid quantitative formula had been adjusted to the available prosodic resources or tendencies in the language, the resulting metric form actually came to have a *dual organizing principle,* syllable length and/or stress. Thus, in a strict sense, one cannot speak of Hungarian iambic meter, for example, as being purely 'quantitative' except by reference to the extra-cultural source of the tradition itself.

Nonetheless, traditional descriptions have treated this verse type on a quantitative basis, i.e., in terms of *that* one of its two ordering principles which is not linguistically—systemically—definable. The present study takes the other alternative and attempts an analysis of an arbitrarily selected corpus of Hungarian iambic verse in the light of the role of stress as a rhythmic principle. In spite of the known fact that in this tradition stress and ictus often do not coincide, the approach taken here is believed to be justified in part on the grounds that the occurrence of stress in general, unlike that of long and short syllables, can be specified by phonological rules, i.e., by a verse-independent and grammar-related description of stress placement in the language, and hence in relation to the speaker's linguistic competence. The distribution of stress as specified by such rules on the one hand, and positions of metric prominence on the other, need not necessarily correspond, as indeed they do not, in order for stress to be shown to be the fundamental linguistic component-feature of Hungarian iambic rhythm; I propose to demonstrate that an explicit characterization of word-stress placement in the language provides a reasonable basis for the formulation of some additional general principles which explain cases of non-correspondence between stress and ictus. Such a stress-oriented notion of iambic meter allows for *a treatment of verse rhythm and the rhythm of ordinary discourse as two manifestations of the same set of underlying prosodic characteristics of the language,* and offers a sound basis in terms of which this affinity can be specified, while it also provides some formal grounds for an identification of the difference between the two rhythm types. So treated, quantitative verse can be discussed in relation to internalized linguistic rules which ultimately determine the 'rhythmic intuition'[13] of poet, reader, and performer alike.

It is to be understood that the present stress-centered approach to Hungarian iambic verse is not meant to question the fundamentally quantitative character of this verse tradition: after all, poets did *intend* to follow, consciously, the quantitative formula, rather than one founded on stress. A verse tradition based on quantity cannot be approached with any hope of success on grounds of a metric theory that assumes an organizing principle other than what poets consciously utilized. To this extent, the view presented here does not represent a true alternative to the quantitative theory. In general, an adequate metric theory is required to provide a basis for identifying the difference between metrical and unmetrical lines within a particular metric tradition, and, furthermore, it must account for all permissable variations among metrically acceptable lines. The present proposal does not meet this requirement; it does not claim to represent an alternate metric theory. What it *is* intended to accomplish rather is to show that syllable length alternation is closely associated with, and often replaced by, stress alternation in fulfilling the metric-rhythmic function. Stated differently, the present study seeks evidence for the hypothesis that while, aside from domestic modifications of borrowed quantitative rules already referred to, poets were *consciously* striving to fill strong metric positions by long syllables *only* by virtue of the length feature of these syllables, they, perhaps subconsciously, associated metric rhythm peaks with the occurrence of syllables that are either stressed or stressable (see Chapter IV). Considerations of stressedness and stressability require that the syllable sequences filling the metric frame be regarded as meaningful grammatical sequences—sentences—rather than as successive occurrences of time units in a structural vacuum of a sort.

The present study relies, in part, on the concept of markedness in accounting for instances in which metrically superimposed rhythmic configurations cannot be explained solely by means of stress rules. The notion of markedness has been used in a somewhat similar sense before.[14] In this analysis, the distinction between metric lines (or parts of lines) in which positions of stress and metric rhythm peaks coincide, on the one hand, and lines (or parts of lines) in which the metrically determined rhythm is in conflict with normal stress contours, on the other, will be regarded as a dichotomy between metrically unmarked and metrically marked occurrences, respectively. Thus unmarked forms are the output of phonological (stress) rules, while marked forms are ones identified as being appropriate only in a particular stylistic (here metric) context but describable in terms of and in relation to the former. Since a chief purpose here is to argue for the pertinence of stress as a metric principle especially in such cases where this role is not immediately obvious (i.e., where stress rules alone are not sufficient for explaining the occurrence of a particular syllable in ictus), attention in this study is centered on metrically marked lines. The analysis given in Chapter IV is expected to show that the accentual behavior of linguistic sequences in such lines can be specified by the same stress placement rule as that which assigns unmarked stress contours, the only necessary adjustment being a modification of the domains of stress placement. To the extent that the basic assumptions and the analytic procedure involved here are plausible, the conclusions reached in this study should suggest a reasonable linguistic view of the status of iambic rhythm in Hungarian verse in relation to prose rhythm in the language. In short, this study attempts to convey evidence for the hypothesis which may be formulated as follows:

$$
\begin{array}{ccccc}
\text{unmarked} & + & \text{metrically marked} & \rightarrow & \text{verse rhythm} \\
\text{stress contours} & & \text{stress contours} & & \text{(iambic)} \\
\uparrow & & \uparrow & & \text{[i.e. correspondence} \\
\text{stress-place-} & & \text{principles of} & & \text{of metric rhythm and} \\
\text{ment rules} & & \text{stressability} & & \text{linguistic rhythm]} \\
\text{(Ch. 3)} & & \text{(Ch. 4)} & &
\end{array}
$$

language-   artificially
inherent   superimposed

Metric formula

The following is intended to define briefly the concept of meter as understood in this study. Successions of lines in a given verse[15] generally display variations of different sorts; in traditional terms, metric feet may be inverted, syllables may be added or deleted, and so on. Such variations imply some norm or standard with respect to which they can be specified: underlying all metric lines is an abstract metric pattern that is relatable to an ideal metric structure or formula.

To illustrate, let us assume that, independent of the particular language that fills it in a given instance, an iambic tetrameter line is defined by a set of metric rules which specify the following abstract properties of the line. The line

(1) has boundaries (( )) at both ends,

(2) consists of a linear sequence of eight syllable *positions* of which

    (a) the first, third, fifth, and seventh are *weak*

    (b) the second, fourth, sixth, and eighth are *strong*

Depending on the analyst's view, a third rule may be added, namely, that

(3) one odd-numbered position and one even-numbered position, in this order, make up a *foot*

The metric rules (1-3) may be illustrated by the following diagram:[16]

(4)

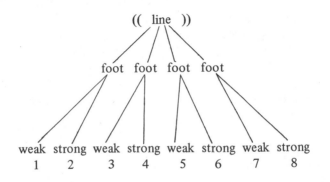

It is abstract frames such as (4) that the poet must fill by meaningful grammatical sequences of his language. More precisely, (4) represents metric *underlying structure*, in this case that of an iambic tetrameter: underlying any line which is acceptable in a particular tradition as an iambic tetrameter there is an abstract metric formula which is derivable from (4). Thus the metric structure of an actual line represents metric *surface structure*. The principal condition for deriving surface forms from underlying forms is that metric equivalence be maintained; hence the class of all iambic tetrameters can be defined as the set of all permissible transformational variants of (4), where transformations are understood in a broad sense to perform changes on arrangements (forms) without affecting perceptual similarity.[17] The set of permissible variations with respect to the underlying formula (4) may vary from language to language within the European metric tradition, although changes such as the inversion of the first and second positions and the addition of an extra-metrical syllable, especially after the last strong position, appear to be universal.[18]

It is assumed, then, that the poet has at his disposal a set of metrically equivalent and perceptually comparable frames which serve as the basis for the selection of sentences as 'fillers'. In particular, he is required, ideally, to fill each strong position of the meter by a *strong* syllable, and each weak position by a syllable that is or can be *weak* in relation to strong syllables. Just what constitutes a weak or strong syllable in a particular language-specific metric tradition is determined, in principle, solely by properties of the linguistic system involved.[19] However, for a syllable to be 'strong' with respect to other syllables, it must be capable of being perceived by speakers of the language as a prominence peak, i.e., it must be, or be associated with, a distinctive entity in the language.

It may be further argued, however, that while the non-distinctiveness of a phonetic feature, such as length in English, is generally both a necessary and sufficient condition for the rejection of that feature as a possible metric principle, it does not follow that phonological distinctiveness as such is a sufficient condition for its acceptance.[20] In a sense this is self-evident since in a sequence of distinctive elements in a metric line only some such elements are capable of signalling metric prominence. But this inference may well be valid in a more specific sense, syllable length in Hungarian being a case in point: length, being phonemic, is suitable for serving as the metric principle in a quantitative verse, although, as we have noted, a syllable need not be long to realize a metric peak. On the other hand, there are convincing reasons for questioning the still fashionable orthodox and musically motivated view, to be reviewed in some detail in the next chapter, that syllable length accomplishes its rhythmic function in quantitative verse without the support of other prosodic features, notably stress, simply because the *quantitative formula does not require* it to be supplemented by them. What the extra-linguistic formula requires is one thing and what the language to which it is applied has available is another; the formula is musically defined but language cannot be so defined, even though both music and language are realized through time. That syllable length is readily available in Hungarian to serve as the quantitative metric principle should not obscure the significant fact that it has another, system-related function, namely, that it is a conditioning factor in low-level stress placement (see Chapter III); thus there is a good case for asserting that if a native audience not only accepts as 'natural' but possibly expects long syllables as metric rhythm peaks, it is on account of the (non-distinctive) *stress* assignable to them due to their length (see Chapter III for details), rather than because of their values as non-linguistic time units. This, at any rate, is the central point of this study.

NOTES

1. Although in principle there is no necessary correlation between verse and poetry (see also footnote 8), in this book verse is understood to imply literary discourse. In this sense, one can speak only of an intersection of linguistics and the study of verse. Some linguists have been careful to recognize the limitations necessarily imposed on all linguistic approaches to the study of literature. Typical is Chatman's warning that linguistics "should play a guarded role in literary analysis. If we do have a tool to hand to the critic, we must realize that it is an auxilliary tool" (1957, p. 239). Somewhat less modest is the rather remarkable claim that literature "cannot be studied with the fullest fruitfulness unless the student is deeply versed in scientific linguistics" (Whitehall and Hill 1964, p. 483). It might be helpful to assume that the language of literature involves a complex of literary, aesthetic, linguistic, psychological, and other factors, and although they are all interrelated, any of these aspects may be fruitfully investigated while all other variables are assumed to be constant.

2. See Saporta 1960, p. 85.

3. For example, Levin 1964, Thorne 1965, and more recent discussions by Chomsky, Levin, Hendricks, Thorne, Bickerton, Hill, and others.

4. As a rule, all linguistic approaches to prosody presuppose that language and meter are two separable components of the metric entity, each with abstract properties of its own. Halle and Keyser regard meter as an "abstract pattern. . . . The poet uses this pattern as a basis of selection so that he may choose out of the infinite number of sentences of natural language those which qualify for inclusion in the poem" (1966, p. 187); J. Lotz notes that "The linguistic study of meter includes two sections, (A) study of the linguistic constituents and (B) study of the metric superstructure" (1960, p. 138). Also cf. Lotz n.d., p. 132; Chatman 1965, p. 96, pp. 103-4; Gáldi 1955, p. 500, Levý 1969, p. 105. Roman Jakobson denies that meter is "an abstract, theoretical scheme" because it has

"many intrinsically linguistic particularities," but he too distinguishes between verse design and "the structure of any single line" which it underlies (1960, pp. 364-5).

5. Halle and Keyser 1966, p. 188.

6. See Hill 1966, and footnote 19 below.

7. Halle and Keyser 1966, p. 191.

8. Although verse is generally associated with poetry since it is an aspect of poetic form, it should be noted that prose may be poetic and verse may well be non-poetic; hence verse and poetry are separate entities.

9. For an excellent programmatic statement on this, see Ohmann 1966.

10. Although the general principles discussed in this study are assumed to be of broader relevance and applicability, only iambic verse has been selected for analysis here because this form came to be the most significant one of all borrowed metric forms in modern Hungarian poetry (see Vargyas 1952, p. 174; Horváth 1955, p. 74). Paradoxically enough, it has also been long felt by scholars that the 'ascending' type of iambic rhythm is inherently incompatible, in part at least, with the 'descending' rhythm of Hungarian. For example, Vargyas refers to "the well-known fact how basically opposed the iambic form is to the nature of Hungarian and how difficult it is to give this form Hungarian flavor" (1952, p. 164). Németh (1963, p. 357) is of a similar opinion, pointing to the lack in Hungarian iambic verse of "a satisfying, unique correspondence" between linguistic and metric rhythm peaks, unlike in English, German, or Russian iambic verse [all translations from Hungarian to English in this study are my own].

The quantitative formulation of metric facts in this verse form in Hungarian gives no basis for a resolution of this paradox: it cannot account for the difference between the artificially superimposed practices and conventions responsible for the partial unnaturalness of iambic rhythm in Hungarian, and, on the other hand, those inherent rhythm features in the language upon which the success of iambic verse rests.

11. The most complete account of the history of the introduction and development of the Greek-Roman metric model in Hungarian is found in Négyesi 1892. A more recent discussion is included in Horváth 1951.

12. This is an oversimplification. The exact prosodic conditions in Greek verse are not known with absolute certainty, and furthermore, there is some evidence that at least some Latin poets did strive to coordinate ictus and stress to a considerable extent. For references, see footnote 5, Chapter II.

13. The term is used here in reference to language, but in discussions on Hungarian verse, particularly by Horváth, it is used in a broader sense: verse rhythm is considered as one manifestation of a larger human need for "rhythmic ordering," also expressed in singing, dancing, as well as other human activities (Horváth 1951, pp. 15-17; for a similar view of rhythm, cf. Zirmunskij 1966). Like all such activities, language too is realized through time; rhythm in language, then, according to Horváth, is a product of the speakers' rhythmic intuition—since "without the involvement of the human mind there can be no rhythmic order" (1951, p. 15)—the very same capacity which enables them to segment other temporal phenomena in the universe into time units.

14. By Lotz, for example, with reference to the Prague School notion of markedness: "verse may be defined by adding to linguic phenomena, the special marks that make verse;. . . verse might be called 'marked' (*merkmalhaft*), prose 'unmarked' (*merkmallos*)" (1942, p. 125).

15. In the sense of 'stanza'. In this study, the metric *line* is taken to be the basic unit of analysis; lines are analyzed into positions (see below) and may be synthesized into higher units such as periods, stanzas, etc.

16. A similar diagram and some of the terminology employed here appear in Keyser 1967.

17. More precisely, transformations relate abstract schemata to physical representation. The notion of transformations as understood here is that discussed in Lenneberg 1967, pp. 298-9. In principle, all similarities involve transformational processes; the concept of grammatical transformations is only one particular utilization of this principle. In metrics, all X-ic (iambic, trochaic, etc.) lines can be conceived of as being transformationally derived from the underlying X-ic schema, which is a common denominator of a sort. This view of metric variations, if plausible, might suggest some psycholinguistic reasons as to why certain variations on a given underlying schema are acceptable and others are not, provided a reasonable definition of 'perceptual similarity' can be formulated. Since metric lines (or certain subsets of the syllable sequence making up a line) can be assumed to be perceived as gestalts (e.g., Lotz 1942, p.

131), several transformational variants of an X-ic schema can function as acceptable X-ic lines without affecting the basic perceptual pattern involved.

18. See Jespersen 1900.

19. It is, of course, possible to create artificial verse in any language in spite of the linguistic system involved, although such verse is not likely to be successful. Lehmann points out that "The Alexandrine has never yielded high poetry in English or German, though it is the common verse pattern in French. . .[while] the use of blank verse is impossible in French. . . .Attempts to introduce into English and German classical meters based on variations in syllabic quantity have failed. . . . When, in late Skaldic verse, speech rhythms and poetic form became incompatible, the form degenerated to a game and had to be sustained by artificial devices" (1956, pp. 65-66). It is now well known that "certain metrical systems are incompatible with some linguistic systems" since "no versification system can be based on prosodic elements which are not relevant in the language" (Stankiewicz 1960, pp. 77-78).

20. For a similar observation, see Lotz 1942, p. 128.

II
THE QUANTITATIVE VIEW

Historically, three main verse traditions in Hungarian literature are generally distinguished, in the following chronological order of appearance: (1) native verse, (2) Classical model, (3) Western European model. Iambic verse belongs to the most recent Western European tradition. Renewed interest and research in the past two decades in problems of Hungarian verse have generated lively debates and substantial disagreements among Hungarian scholars particularly on prosodic aspects of native rhythm and of the iambic form. The key issue appears to be the relation of verse rhythm to rhythm in ordinary discourse, and specifically the role of stress in verse with respect to the time-defined abstract structure of the latter. In general, the disagreements boil down to the problem whether the behavior of sentences—syllable sequences—in verse frames is basically a musical or a linguistic phenomenon.

This controversy has been centered partly around the views of János Horváth, by far the most influential expert on Hungarian verse during the past four decades. Horváth has been the foremost advocate of the musical quantitative concept of verse in Hungarian.[1] So far as native verse is concerned, this concept has been disputed, on various grounds, by linguistically oriented scholars in the past few decades,[2] and several have expressed doubt recently concerning Horváth's position on metrics as well.[3]

The present chapter is intended to examine briefly some basic assumptions of the quantitative view regarding the borrowed Western European model in general and iambic verse in particular. The origins of this tradition in Hungarian are well documented: the traveller Gedeon Ráday first introduced the model in the 1730's from Germany, and henceforth this model came to be called 'Ráday-type'.[4] At that time, the previously borrowed and apparently strictly *quantitative* Classical Greek-Roman model[5] was flourishing in Hungarian literature; now Ráday implanted the originally same metric model from a language in which the classical organizing principle of length had been replaced by *stress*. Since, then, the Western model was strictly stress-based, it might be supposed that the model metric principle would be, if not necessarily adopted indiscriminately, at least absorbed in some way into the metric system finally established in the borrowing language.

Horváth denies this possibility. He argues that the metric organizing principle adopted for the 'Western tradition' in Hungarian was modelled after the classical quantitative formula already fashionable in Hungary in the early eighteenth century, rather than after the stress-based principle prevalent in the Western source language. He maintains, in fact, that the metric measuring principle developed in the Hungarian tradition "was rendered *completely* (emphasis added) independent of stress conditions in the language" and "left the freedom of stress untouched. . . from the beginning."[6] Thus, in iambic verse in particular, "stress can freely fulfill its natural function, which is to make prominent by loudness certain contentive (semantic, emotive) elements of speech."[7]

Indeed the dislocation of semantically motivated stress with respect to strong metric positions is common in Hungarian iambic verse, and there is no reason to suppose that, in general, poets consciously attempted to co-ordinate stress—distinctive stress—and ictus; on the contrary, they seem to have strived to comply to varying degrees with the rigid quantitative rules that came to be accepted, and did so often at the expense of forcing rather artificial and counter-intuitive superimpositions of the iambic frame on normal linguistic stress contours. It cannot be claimed, then, that the base of this verse form is (distinctive) stress in Hungarian, as is the case in the Germanic languages, for example. What may well be open to question, however, is the tenability of the implied assertion that iambic verse became a successful expressive form in Hungarian literature by virtue of its musical-quantitative character irrespective of the inherent *linguistic* relationship of syllable quantity to other abstract rhythmic components of the language, notably stress.

Evidently, in asserting the lack of any correlation between stress and metric prominence, Horváth and his followers mean by 'stress' only linguistically functional (i.e., semantically motivated) distinctive stress (see Chapter III for details). Thus one cannot reasonably argue that in terms of their own concept of stress their interpretation of the role of stress, or rather of its lack of any role, in iambic verse is false. What quantitative theorists fail to recognize, however, is the fact that the distribution of stress in the language is not limited to semantically motivated stresses, and that actually the syllables bearing distinctive stress are only a relatively small subset of the total number of syllables which receive some degree of stress within a given unit of discourse. Furthermore, these other, linguistically non-functional low-degree stresses can be shown to be a basic component of rhythm in ordinary speech;[8] as a matter of fact, their contribution to the generation of speech rhythm may be their only funtion. Proponents of the quantitative view fail to give a reason why, as they seem to imply, a basic rhythmic element in normal, non-metric manifestations of language should somehow cease to be relevant to the rhythm of linguistic sequences in a metric frame. The principal fallacy in this view is the faulty inference that since distinctive stress is irrelevant to the metric principle, therefore all stress is irrelevant.

It seems that this denial of the necessity for a syllable, short *or* long, to have a certain degree of stress in order to realize a metric rhythm peak is a result of a confusion of the nature of the metric formula and rhythmic potentials of the linguistic sequences that fill it. One cannot accept the proposition that the fact that the metric *formula* in question, which originated in a culture where verse was closely related to music, is or can be defined by the principle of regular time measurement should be taken to imply that rhythm in a *natural language* is necessarily subject to definition by the same rigid principle. It is readily granted that the iambic frame ideally requires a temporally (musically) specified quantitative metric principle; musically, the time continuum can be segmented into successive units of any length, and if sets of comparable time-units regularly alternate through time, certainly the result is some sort of a rhythm regardless of whether other physical features such as loudness or pitch participate in this alternation. The metric frame (cf. [4] in Chapter I) is simply an abstract representation of a portion of the time continuum; within the frame, abstract time is divided into a set of (equally) short units and a set of (equally) long units, and particular arrangements of these units define different types of verse (iambic, trochaic, anapestic, etc.). By convention, rhythmic peaks are supposed to be marked by positions of long time units. It follows from this concept of meter that the entity which is to fill this abstract frame must be realizable through time; but it does *not* follow that this entity—language—will be rhythmically actualized necessarily by the same principle as that defining the formula. Even in a language where speakers can perceive length distinctions and syllable length is accepted as the organizing principle, length as a component of linguistic rhythm cannot be separated from stress of some degree, which generally accompanies it or co-occurs with it.[9]

The claim discussed here enjoys substantial support by Fónagy, a leading authority on stress. Fónagy argues, in disagreement with Horváth, that in Hungarian, just like in German, English, Russian, etc., syllables in strong metric position are pronounced *louder,* whether they are long or short, with respect to those in weak position. He correctly points out that even

> in the so-called time-measured (quantitative) Hungarian verse the meter cannot be animated without the support of stress. It is the arrangement of those long syllables that are made prominent, and not of those neutral with respect to prominence, that brings about the sense of motion which forms the basis of our rhythmic intuition. Time-measured units are not capable of

accomplishing this *for the very reason that their own occurrence depends to a large extent on positions of stress* (emphasis provided).[10]

In reference to experimental evidence cited by him elsewhere,[11] Fónagy further notes that in ordinary speech in Hungarian, the objectively measured duration of short stressed vowels often equals the duration of unstressed long vowels. Thus a native speaker does not intuitively consider a short stressed syllable to be an appropriate filler of a weak metric position with respect to an unstressed long syllable in strong position: the meter-determined rhythm can be assured only by subduing the linguistic stress on the former "by artistic means": there would be "no need for such manipulation if time-measured meter, the alternation of (linguistically) long and short syllables, could, without the support of stress, enable the listener to experience" the intended rhythm.[12]

Fónagy's observation points in the right direction but it does not go far enough: of real linguistic interest is not so much the necessity for a metrically prominent syllable to be supplemented by some degree of stress in actual *performance,* but rather the question whether this stress is linguistically justifiable and whether its occurrence is related to and definable in terms of the *system of stress placement* in the language.

The hypothesis that in general there exists such a correlation is in the focus of attention in this paper: it is not diametrically opposed to the quantitative interpretation of the iambic verse form in Hungarian, but rather assumes a yet uninvestigated linguistic basis for the success of the quantitative principle. On the other hand, this aim requires that one re-examine the principal basis on which the quantitative theory is founded: namely, that pre-defined abstract verse rhythm has priority over, and prevails indiscriminately in spite of, linguistically given rhythm. Horváth asserts that once the reader or listener becomes familiar with a metric pattern—as Hungarians needed "to get used to"[13] the iambic form—he will come to expect it: "the number, kind, and order of time units (Hungarian *ütem*) are determined *a priori* and are established in the mind in advance. . . striving to be realized by speech without being altered." The "original vitality" of the abstract rhythmic plan is then supposed to be so great that this plan "is actualized irrespective of speech" and can impose itself "even on meaningless stretches of discourse."[14] That discrepancy between metric rhythm and speech rhythm should occur in verse is not unusual; variations of this sort are a chief poetic tool for the conveyance of intensity of feeling, emphasis, etc., and are common in metric traditions. What is remarkable about this notion of quantitative verse, however, is that it claims such discrepancies to be normal, rather than to be exceptions. Even if non-correspondence between sense and rhythm is granted to be the norm, one fails to find a reasoned *explanation* in the quantitative theory as to why metric language in successful iambic verse is not reduced to 'accentual gibberish' of some sort and is readily accepted by a native audience as in general not being inconsistent with prosodic constraints in the language.

Quantitative rules[15]

The rules defining classical quantitative meter are familiar to students of European metrics: the portion of the time-continuum represented by a metric line is divided into time-units (feet), and each such unit is further segmented into sub-units which may be short or long (the time value ratio being 1 to 2). The iambic line is characterized by a succession of time-units each of which contains one short and one long sub-unit, in this order. Each sub-unit is linguistically manifested by a syllable, and therefore one can speak of an iambic line as being a succession of short and long syllables, marking rhythmic valleys and rhythmic peaks, respectively.

The first step in the study of prosody is to establish what syllables 'count' as short or long. Hungarian prosodists accepted the Greek-Roman notion of syllable,[16] briefly defined as follows:

short syllable: $V \; (C^1)$

long syllable: $\left\{ \begin{array}{l} \bar{V} \; (C_0) \\ V \; C_2 \end{array} \right\}$

That is, a short vowel or a short vowel followed by no more than one (single) consonant represents a short syllable, and a long vowel with or without any following consonant(s) or a short vowel followed by at least two (single) consonants (or a double consonant) makes up a long syllable. In a purely quantitative sense, then, line 159 is a 'perfect' iambic line[17] since each strong position is occupied by a long syllable and each weak position is filled by a short syllable (the line number refers to the Text in the Appendix):

159. a ta:ršaša:gban e:n iš ott vale:k*
     *A Table of Symbols is given on p. 91.

where the underlined syllables are those in ictus. By convention, also adopted from classical metrics, a short syllable may 'act' as a long syllable if it precedes a major pause, such as the end of a line (141) or a caesura (marked by /, 88), for

in such cases the time value of the pause is supposed to supplement the duration
of the short vowel:

> 88. š hahogy sabad / amit jövendöl hinnem

> 141. ha:t a ciga:ny / vacog foga

The metric prominence of the short syllables ad (88) and a (line-final, 141) is
thus supposed to be achieved strictly on a time-basis, irrespective of stress.
Similarly, the iambic rhythm in line 159 is said to be realized primarily by the
regular alternation of short and long time units, and the fact that there is a
one-one correspondence between ictus and stress is taken to be a pure
coincidence.[18]
Let us further consider the following lines:

> 86. oh haldoklo: e:v / ši:rod mellett engem

> 156. ši:rhalma:t kereši a temetö:ben

In line 156, three of the five strong positions are occupied by short syllables,
even though in none of the cases is there a following boundary (pause).[19] Yet,
by Hungarian metric standards, the line is regular: because of the frequency of
short stressed syllables in the language, Hungarian prosodists introduced as a
domestic modification of the quantitative formula a rule allowing the 'substitution' of the first (stressed) syllable of a polysyllabic word for an expected long
syllable in strong position. Thus ker and tem in 156 are supposed to be made
prominent with respect to neighboring syllables by being stressed, rather than by
length. For the same reason, short monosyllables came to be acceptable as
substitutes for syllable length in ictus. The monosyllabic article a (141) is a
special case of this convention.[20]
The permissibility of short stressed syllables in ictus implies that length is
not a necessary condition for a syllable to be metrically prominent. Line 86
demonstrates that length is in fact not even a sufficient condition. Note that in
this line, as in countless others, both strong *and* weak positions are filled by long
syllables (i.e., the line is made up of five spondees). The obvious iambic rhythm
in such instances cannot be explained on grounds on short-long syllable
alternation. What, then, distinguishes one long syllable from the other? Again,
the quantitative explanation breaks down: Horváth himself admits that in such
instances it is "*only* (emphasis added) the successive occurrences of stress that

make one sense the iambic rhythm."[21] Incidentally, the frequency with which such long-syllable sequences occur apparently far exceeds Horváth's estimate.[22]

In brief, the quantitative theory interprets the role of stress in this metric form as follows:

A. Stress is *necessary* for (a) the short first syllable of a polysyllabic word and (b) a short monosyllable (except if followed by a pause) to be in ictus.

B. Stress is *necessary* for distinguishing metrically prominent long syllables from adjacent metrically neutral long syllables.

C. Stress is *incidental* to (permissible and 'welcome', but not required on) (a) the long first syllable of a polysyllabic word and (b) a long monosyllable in ictus.

D. A stressed syllable may occur in any weak position. Hence in all cases except those in A and B, stress is metrically *irrelevant;* the metric prominence of any non-first syllable is realized exclusively by quantitative means, i.e., by either (a) a long syllable in ictus or (b) a supplementation of the duration of a short syllable in ictus by the time value of a following pause.

The following Table summarizes the permissible (+) occurrence of the four possible syllable types, with respect to the two possible metric positions:

Syllable	Permissible metric position	
	Strong	Weak
Long stressed	+	+
Long unstressed	+	+
Short stressed	+	+
Short unstressed	−	+

In his classic paper on the role of stress in borrowed versification systems in Hungarian literature (see footnote 15), Horváth presents substantial evidence in support of this theory. He groups some 315 iambic lines, carefully selected

from the works of forty-seven Hungarian poets, into four major categories by
the following criteria:

I. (122 lines), foot structure: o -́. This group is said to demonstrate the
"support of metrically prominent long syllables by occasionally co-occurring
stress" (C above). Three of the 122 lines are an addenda to illustrate (B).

II. (53 lines), foot structure: ō ó. "Short stressed syllables in ictus" (A
above).

III. (116 lines), foot structure: ó -. "Short stressed syllables in weak
positions" (D above).

IV. (24 lines), foot structure: ō̇ ō. "Counter-iambic stress sequences" (D
above).

Let us briefly examine some points in Horváth's argument. His claim,
reflected in I, that in cases of the co-occurrence of length and stress the former is
somehow primary and the latter is secondary (or even incidental) as the basic
rhythmic component is clearly arbitrary, and appears to testify to an
unquestioning and uncritical adherence to the traditional interpretation of this
verse form. This assertion is in want of linguistic evidence in its support. That, in
fact the opposite may well be the case is shown in II where non-long syllables
mark rhythmic prominence *solely* by virtue of being stressed. In contrast, the
foot types included in the categories III and IV are presented as strong
counter-evidence to a stress-based interpretation: in all these foot structures the
linguistically motivated rhythmic peaks, signalled by the positions of stress, are
dislocated with respect to the rhythmic configuration of the meter. At the same
time, in IV at least, the syllable structure may be *any* combination of two
syllables regardless of length distinction. If in these cases neither stress nor
regular short-long syllable alternation is to assure the iambic rhythm, how, one
wonders, is this rhythmic pattern to be realized at all? According to Horváth,
wherever the syllable structure of an iambic foot in an actual line of verse is not
an exact image of (i.e., does not bear a one-one correspondence to) the ideal
(one short-one long) formula, the 'rhythmic impulse' represented by the latter
takes over and thus maintains the regular rhythmic flow which the mind is
predisposed to perceive (cf. footnote 14). It follows then that in this
interpretation not only is the distribution of linguistically defined stresses
immaterial to a discussion of metric rhythm, but so is the actual syllabic
composition of a given verse line. Indeed as long as one persistently maintains
that the rhythm of versified stretches of discourse is strictly a temporal-musical
phenomenon and therefore must be treated in terms of an alternation of
time-units, one can cherish little hope that such discourse can be subjected to

rigorous linguistic analysis and its basic affinity to the rest of language can be shown.

Are the examples which Horváth cites under III and IV really in strong support of the contention that the linguistic realization of iambic rhythm in Hungarian is basically independent of stress? Can one accept the proposition that, insofar as rhythmic potentials are concerned, when in a metric frame sentences somehow cease to function as sentences and disintegrate instead into a mechanical, linear sequence of time-measured syllables? Furthermore, is there a true conflict between assuming that rhythmic properties of ordinary discourse must be the basis of metric analysis, and, on the other hand, postulating an abstract time-defined mental formula of meter as a guiding principle with respect to which the rhythmic behavior of the linguistic material is to be judged? I think not; the very lack of perfect correspondence between the two superimposed rhythmic configurations is a key identifying criterion for metric verse, and the 'tension' which the interplay of the two patterns produces is in general of significant literary and esthetic value. If the syllable sequences making up a metric line are to carry the label 'language', then they must be treated as such: they must be considered as units of meaningful discourse—sentences or parts of sentences with linguistically *predictable* rhythmic characteristics. A central task of metric study is to specify the ways in which the extra-linguistic meter 'stretches' and 'twists' the linguistically given rhythm of the filling language material, and hence renders it deviant. A specification of the nature of this deviance ultimately amounts to a definition of 'verse rhythm' (i.e., the behavior of versified language), as opposed to 'prose rhythm'.

Such considerations do not enter into Horváth's analysis. In the quantitativist formulation, the concept of metrically relevant language amounts to a 'succession of syllables'. Grammatical structure, for example, as a partial determiner of positions of stress (and hence of rhythm) has no place in this theory. It is thus understandable that in attempting to show the lack of any relationship between prominent metric positions and meaning-signalling stresses in the examples under III and IV, Horváth makes no reference to the conditions under which the given stressed syllables occur in weak metric position (e.g., is the stress weak in relation to another stress within the same constituent, is the stressed syllable preceded by a major syntactic break, is the syllable a monosyllable, etc.), and does not consider the possibility of assuming a formal basis for his indication of positions of stress. He does not acknowledge the existence of low-level stresses within words, and since "we do not all place stress alike," even of the high-level, semantically functional stresses he marks "only the most certain ones."[23] Aside from the fact that several cases which he judges to be 'certain' may not be certain at all,[24] the principle underlying Horváth's procedure is subjective and hence essentially invulnerable.

The plausibility of a stress-oriented interpretation of the metric lines included in groups III and IV cannot be objectively judged, then, in the light of Horváth's concept of stress. Let us assume for the moment, however, that his indication of occurrences of stress is generally correct. In these two groups, 262 syllables are marked by stress (in weak metric position). A rough examination of positions of the stressed syllables reveals the following (here I anticipate some points to be discussed in detail in later chapters): in 56 per cent of the cases (147 instances) the stressed syllable immmediately follows a major boundary (and in an additional fourteen instances a minor categorical boundary). Monosyllables make up 8 per cent, syllables immediately preceded by a monosyllable 12 per cent, and verb stems preceded by a verbal prefix 4 per cent. Furthermore, in about 8 per cent of the cases stress can be shown, by reference to pertinent stress placement rules of the language, to be weak with respect to stress on the preceding word, and hence naturally susceptible to and available for reduction when the metric rhythm so requires. The relevance of these facts will be made clear in subsequent chapters; it should suffice to point out here that Horváth's corpus, which represents a historical cross-section of this verse tradition, is generally consistent with and supports the conclusions of this study.

One more comment is in order regarding the so-called "counter-iambic stress sequences," illustrated by group IV.[25] Horváth builds his case against stress around the considerable number of lines which contain at least one strong linguistic stress in weak position. In all such cases the iambic formula requires that the point of prominence be shifted to the next syllable on the right, which often happens to be a syllable that in ordinary discourse is never stressed. Such prominence shift is clearly artificial linguistically speaking, although it can be learned and accepted as a characteristic verse-specific usage. But in a great many cases even a failure to submit to the force of the mechanical formula and to realized the prominence shift, is of negligibly adverse rhythmic consequence. The cases in question are especially those at the beginning of a line; if here and there in the first hemistich a strong linguistic stress makes a syllable in neutral metric position prominent, the metrically determined rhythm can quickly re-establish itself and still enable the listener to experience the iambic nature of the line. Jespersen points out in his classic study of meter, for example, that in general "deviations from the ordinary pattern are always best tolerated in the beginning of the verse (i.e., line), because then there is still time to return to the regular movement."[26] In iambic verse this is true of the first foot, though not of the second. Thus in cases of what may be the most common place for discrepancy between stress and ictus in Hungarian iambic lines, namely the first two metric positions, rhythmic dislocation is not a serious matter, nor is the counter-iambic effect of the position of stress significant. What *is* of crucial rhythmic as well as linguistic interest, however, is the manner in which after such rhythmic breaks the resumption of the regular iambic movement is realized: there seems to be good reason to believe that the strong tendency of the metric pattern to maintain itself is supported primarily and basically by the successive occurrence of either stressed or stressable syllables[27] in strong metric positions. So far as normal stress occurrence is concerned, this thesis does not flatly contradict or deny the quantitativist notion that rhythmic peaks are generally realized by long syllables; it shows, rather, that syllable length can fulfill this function chiefly because it tends to be correlated with the distribution of stress under certain conditions. The concept of stressability, on the other hand, requires a loosening of some of the constraints on stress placement in the language, and thus provides for an enlarging of the domain within which normal stress rules operate. As a result, normally unstressed syllables in strong metric position can be assigned metrically motivated stress in a systematic manner and on the basis of the same general principles which operate in ordinary stress distribution. These matters are discussed in detail in the following two chapters.

NOTES

1. An extensive bibliography on the history of quantitative prosody in Hungarian is included in Horváth 1951. Kecskés 1966, includes an updated critical survey of approaches to the problem of rhythm in Hungarian verse. Most of the discussion in this chapter is based on Horváth's writings, but is directed toward the strict quantitative theory as a whole.

2. Especially Hegedűs 1934, Gábor 1952, Vargyas 1952 (of which 1966 is a revised version) and Szabédi 1955. (The linguistic merits of the latter work are, incidentally, somewhat obscured by its ideological orientation. It is not without difficulty that one can appreciate, if at all, the linguistic significance of Szabédi's interpretation of the distinction between the quantitative and linguistic views of verse rhythm as one between the socio-political philosophies of idealism and materialism, respectively.)

3. For example, Németh 1963, pp. 399-405; Fónagy 1959, pp. 131-2.

4. Horváth 1951, p. 138. For details, see Négyesi 1898.

5. To what extent this model was purely quantitative at the time of its introduction in Hungary is unclear. There are some indications that in Latin verse at least, which was the direct source for the classical model, poets strived to coordinate ictus and stress, especially in the second hemistich. Sturtevant's statistical studies show a correlation between stress on isolated words and ictus in 72 per cent of the complete lines examined; in the last two feet in Virgil's hexameter he found a correlation of 99, 5 per cent of the cases (1940, p. 211; also cf. Fónagy 1959, p. 132). Similar conclusions are drawn in duBois 1906. Fónagy also calls attention to the testimony of Quintilian that in the reading of verse stress shifts to the syllable in ictus. It would be difficult to imagine that such tendencies in the model verse tradition had no influence on prosody in the borrowing language.

6. 1955, p. 72.

7. 1955, p. 78.

8. In addition to other features such as pause, pitch, and syllable length. Pause (grammatical and morphological boundaries) and syllable length are related to stress distribution in the language, although, as already noted, syllable length is not a necessary condition for the occurrence of stress. Pitch generally coincides with stress in indicative sentences but not necessarily in others.

It might be noted here in passing that pitch appears to be immaterial to the metric principle in Hungarian iambic verse although, of course, physically and perceptually it is one of the components of rhythm (see Fónagy 1959, and Kecskés 1966, regarding Hungarian); a syllable rendered prominent by high pitch, such as one of the last two syllables in an interrogative sentence, may or may not be in strong metric position. In line 183 in the Text (see Appendix), *é:lék? ném é:lek?* 'Am I alive? Am I not alive?', stress (in weak positions) and pitch (in strong positions) do not coincide, and in fact pitch rather than stress assures the iambic rhythm; on the other hand, in line 102, *égyma:ßt válaha* 'each other again?', the syllable bearing pitch is in weak position and goes counter to the stress-governed metric rhythm. Such cases where stress and pitch do not coincide are extremely rare and even then have no metric significance. (But cf. footnote 3, Chapter IV.)

9. The nature of this correlation in Hungarian is discussed in detail in Chapter III.

10. 1959, p. 131.

11. 1958, p. 15, for example.

12. 1959, p. 131. Fónagy does not state but clearly implies that in addition to subduing distinctive stress on the syllable in weak position, it is also necessary to give a certain degree of phonetic stress to the long syllable in strong position.

13. 1955, p. 76. "The Hungarian rhythmic instinct needed practice so that it could appropriately react to this 'musical floating' [of iambic verse] so totally new and so foreign to it, and that it could accept and judge this form by virtue of a mentally expected ideal formula, the same way as it anticipates the

pattern of native verse." It may be universally true that, in this sense, *any* verse formula (other than perhaps that developed out of native rhythm) needs to be 'learned' or 'accustomed to'; furthermore, it may be possible for speakers of a given language to learn and come to expect just about any formula, artificial as it may be. The point is not that the 'musical floating' of iambic *meter* could be accepted, but that the language was capable of being adjusted to a large extent to the requirements of this form: the basis for this adjustment, as this study attempts to demonstrate, was the poets' and readers' intuitive association of rhythmic peaks with the occurrence of some form of stress.

14. The foregoing quotations from Horváth are taken from Szabédi 1955, p. 51, line 53 where references are not given. Incidentally, this concept of the relationship between meter and language is very much like that advanced for Chaucer's iambic verse by B. Ten Brink (1901) for example; for a refutation of this view, see Halle and Keyser 1966, esp. pp. 188-189.

15. The main source for the following discussion is Horváth 1955, the most comprehensive statement on the quantitativist position on stress so far published.

16. The term 'syllable' is commonly used in reference to Hungarian in a somewhat different sense as well which may be defined by the following:

$$\#\#(C_0) \quad V \left\{ \begin{matrix} \left\{ \begin{matrix} (/C) \\ C \ /C \ (C) \end{matrix} \right\} \\ (C) \ /\#\# \end{matrix} \right\} \quad V$$

where $\#\#$ is a sentence boundary and / is syllable boundary. That is, following a sentence boundary, the first syllable includes the first vowel, all (if any) preceding consonants, and the first of at least two following consonants. A following single consonant belongs to the first syllable before a sentence boundary and to the next syllable before a vowel. This syllabification process may operate across word boundaries, over phrases, up to sentence (see Balassa 1887, pp. 405-6). For example, $\#\#ve{:}g/re/{-}it/t{-}a/{-}ta/vas\#\#$ 'spring is here at last', where - marks word boundary.

17. Lines of this syllable structure are relatively rare; in the text analyzed here (see Appendix) they constitute only about 3 to 5 per cent of the lines.

18. This point is repeatedly made in Horváth 1955. For example: "While stress is left free to fulfill its linguistic-semantic function without any rhythmic constraints whatever, certain positionally fixed rhythmic values may gain support by intensity [through stress] which *accidentally* (emphasis provided] happens to co-occur with them" (p. 78); "The linguistic intuition which domesticated the foreign iambic model left stress in its natural syntactic domain, not even expecting that *here and there* thereby it would allocate *occasional* (emphases provided) additional energy to its otherwise lurking time measurement" (p. 95; the translation is as close as possible).

19. It is not clear whether the syllable *i* in *kereši* (line 156) violates the Hungarian quantitative principle as formulated by early prosodists. The problem is whether a pause after *i* is justified. There *is* a constituent boundary at this point between the verb *kereši* and the place adverbial phrase *a temetö:ben,* but whether this is a sufficiently 'high-level' boundary to justify a pause of the sort before which prosodists accepted a short syllable in ictus for reasons already noted, appears to be an open question. If the line is analyzed in stress terms, this issue does not arise since the syllable *i* is assigned normal secondary stress (see Chapter III), and therefore its occurrence in strong position is perfectly legitimate, 'rhythmically' speaking.

20. Since other stressable (see Chapter IV) but normally unstressed short monosyllables are accepted in ictus solely by virtue of the stress they can receive (even though this stress may not be distinctive!), it is difficult to understand Horváth's speculation that the definite article *a* as well as the demonstrative pronoun *e* "indeed can be pronounced either short or long," and hence either time value may be used "as the need dictates" (1955, p. 71). It is true that, historically, *a* for example, developed from *az* (the two variants are now in context-determined distribution); thus *a ciga:ny* (line 141) ⟵ *ac ciga:ny* ⟵ *az ciga:ny,* and this process was complete only about a hundred years ago (see Hegedüs 1959, p. 108). Yet it is still not clear how *a* without stress, even if long, can signal a metric rhythm peak, especially where a strongly stressed long syllable occurs in the following weak position (e.g., lines 80, 116, 121, 123, etc.). For a discussion of some linguistically pertinent questions regarding the definite article *a*, see Vargyas 1952, p. 252.

21. 1955, p. 80.

22. At least in the text examined here, no more than 5 per cent of the lines do *not* contain one or more sequences of at least three long syllables where

clearly only stress assures the iambic rhythm. Horváth considers only lines of the syllable structure of line 86 which occur, as he correctly points out, only sporadically. But if only stress can make prominent one long syllable with respect to adjacent long syllables *throughout* a line such as 86, is it not reasonable to suppose that shorter sequences of long syllables are subject to the same stress function?

23. 1955, p. 78.

24. One difficulty in discussing Horváth's examples is that his corpus consists of individual lines taken out of context, and it cannot be determined with certainty whether or not he takes the context into consideration in stressing some words but not others. Yet the larger conceptual context, the knowledge of 'preceding information'(cf. p. 34), appears to be crucial to correct accentuation in Hungarian (as no doubt in other languages as well). It can only be in relation to the preceding context, if at all, that the first word in *š néved fog e:lni tu:l idö:kön* 'and your náme will live beyond the times' can receive (emphatic) stress, for example, and one does not necessarily share Horváth's certainty in assigning major stress to words such as *tála:n* 'perhaps', *hánem* 'but', or *mídö:n* 'whilst' (pp. 84-86), even in their respective contexts.

25. It might be pointed out that Horváth does not consider the foot structure in III 'counter-iambic' because Hungarians, he argues, pronounce a short stressed syllable in a quick, snapping manner, and as a result of this "pure Magyar pronunciation" the duration of the following long syllable will even (perceptually) be increased, thus promoting the iambic rhythm. For evidence to the contrary, see Fónagy 1959, p. 131 (cf. footnote 12).

26. 1900, p. 73.

27. Particularly by the occurrence of 'non-distinctive', secondary word stresses, which appear to have no reality for 'timers'. It is perhaps a matter of opinion to what extent one may grant, as Horváth does (inadvertently?), that stress has a significant metric function in this verse tradition and still insist that the rhythmic principle employed is inherently stress-free. The catch-word in this paradox may be 'substitution': substituted feet are irregular and somehow only 'second best' with respect to the time-units that should ideally occur in their place if the rhythm is to be realized through regular time-unit alternation. The difficulty with the concept of substitution is that, in this tradition at least, substituted feet are far too common for the time-defined rhythm to be

actualized in spite of them, and their number may in fact exceed that of regular units in some poems. A statistical survey of Horváth's 312 lines reveals, for example, that no less than 32 per cent of the first four weak positions contain irregular long syllables (between two adjacent long syllables), and nearly 10 per cent of the first four strong positions are occupied by short syllables. If we should add to the unquestioned function of stress in all these instances all its admitted 'supporting' roles, we might find that, statistically, the alternate presence and absence of stress figures in the realization of more rhythmic units than does the alternation of 'pure' time-units.

III
STRESS

Jakobson and Halle point out in *Fundamentals of Language* that "languages where both length and stress appear as distinctive features are quite exceptional."[1] This essentially disjunctive relation between distinctive length and stress exists, among other languages, in English where only stress is distinctive, and, on the other hand, in Hungarian where the distribution of stress is rather limited but all phonological segments are distinguished along the axis of length.[2] If *word* and *sentence* are taken to be two basic domains of stress occurrence, and the stress configurations of these domains are labelled *word stress* and *sentence stress* (accent), respectively, then it may be said that in Hungarian sentence stress is distinctive and word stress is non-distinctive. Functionally, this distinction might be viewed as a dichotomy between *linguistically* motivated and *rhythmically* motivated stress contours, since the former reflect the meaning—the semantic interpretation—of a sentence, while the latter have as their primary (and possibly sole) function the avoidance of long sequences of unstressed syllables between accents, and hence of monotony of speech.[3] Since the existence and basic rhythmic function of lesser stresses in ordinary discourse in Hungarian is no longer a matter of dispute, it is rather surprising that while the language of meter has been traditionally claimed to utilize the "inherent rhythm"[4] of the language as a whole, a basic component of that rhythm—stress—has been generally ignored in metric studies.

To provide a linguistic basis for the analysis presented in the latter part of this study, in this chapter we shall examine the distribution of non-distinctive, rhythmically-motivated stresses in Hungarian. In the way of preliminaries to this discussion, we will assume the *sentence* and its syntactically defined constituents to be the basic units of stress description.[5] In principle, the domain to which accents are to be assigned provides information (e.g., in the form of labelled bracketing) on the categorial and syntactic status of the constituents within its bounds. Thus given a sentence, or, more properly, a major constituent such as a noun phrase or verb phrase, the speaker can place accents of various degrees within the domain by his knowledge of the constituent structure and of the accent rule that applies to it, in addition to certain kinds of semantic information. There are general rules in the language, such as

(1) in a modifier-modified phrase, the modifier receives (stronger) accent.
(2) the constituent immediately preceding the predicate receives (stronger) accent.

Whether, in a particular instance, the constituent not having the strong accent also receives a lower-degree accent appears to depend on such factors as the following:

(a) *word length:* of two noun phrases such as *jo: ember* 'good man' and *serenče:tlen fiatalember* 'unfortunate young man', the noun *fiatalember* has a weak accent apparently solely on account of the length of the whole construction (for position of accent, see below), whereas the noun *ember* in the first example is not affected by this condition.[6]

(b) *semantic importance:* a constituent is accented if it is logically important. In fact, the principles expressed in (1) and (2) have been recognized traditionally only as tendencies; for

> any syntactic constituent may be accented or unaccented, depending on the function it fulfills in the course of speech: whether it provides new information, or whether it refers to a previous statement or is a self-evident circumstance.[7]

Some eighty years ago, Balassa described Hungarian stress on similar grounds, by the criterion of ''what the speaker considers important.''[8] For example, in discussing noun phrases of the constituent structure *adjective – noun* (cf. [1]), Balassa notes that if the adjective serves "to narrow the (semantic) range, i.e., change the meaning of," the noun, then the noun is unaccented; on the other hand, when the adjective does not affect the meaning of the noun but serves "merely for circumscription, decoration," then the noun is also accented.[9] Other categories are described on the same (semantic) basis. Balassa's classic study apparently has not been superseded by any subsequent description of Hungarian stress, in substance at least,[10] even though, at least in the example cited, the borderline between his two semantic subcategories is unclear and several of his examples are open to doubt.[11]

Although, evidently, an up-dated systematic characterization, on formal grounds, of Hungarian accentuation is yet to be worked out, the present unavailability of such a description with a degree of *predictive* power will not affect the assumptions to be made in this study. Because of the nature of the verse tradition being analyzed, in which the meaning-signalling function of distinctive stress is subordinated to the rhythmic function of non-distinctive stress, and hence accented syllables often fill weak positions, it is immaterial for the present purpose whether or not we know the precise conditions which determine accent placement *uniquely*. Accordingly, it will be sufficient to establish which constituents are *accentable* under certain *syntactic* conditions (rather than which ones *must* be accented). It will be assumed, for example, that

> (3) within the domains of (1) and (2), the first constituent or both constituents are accentable.

(3) expresses the generalization that both members of a determinant-determined relation may be strongly stressed (on the sentence level), although the "determinant has a stronger tendency to receive strong stress."[12]

Once the constituent to be assigned accent is known, the exact position of accent *within* the domain of the constituent is specified by the *primary word stress* rule, namely,

> (4) primary word stress is invariably on the first syllable.

Hence accent invariably occurs on the first syllable of the constituent word. The relation between accent and primary word stress is, of course, not reciprocal since it is not the case that all first syllables within a domain are necessarily accented. But let us suppose for the moment that every first syllable within a phrase carries an accent of some degree such as in (5) and (6) where the accent contours are assigned by (1) and (2), respectively, and (a) on page 34 is taken into account:

> (5) ##NP [[fégyelmezetlen] AJ [gyèrek] N] NP##
> 'undisciplined child'
> (6) ##VP [[kéllemetlenek] AJ [vàgytok] V] VP##
> 'you [pl.] are unpleasant'

where ´ and ` mark strong and weak accent, respectively. (5) and (6) show the limit to which accent rules apply; appropriate accents having been placed on a syntactic-semantic basis (and in the light of factors such as [a]), the *grammatically* defined bounds within which accent rules operate become irrelevant. Further stress distinctions—the distribution of non-distinctive lower-degree word stresses—are specified by *secondary word stress* rules that apply to sequences of syllables between two accents, which may constitute one or more words. For easier exposition we will temporarily assume that the domain of secondary word stress rules is a single word. Word stress placement is conditioned by *phonological* and *positional* factors, as will be shown, and is independent of constituent structure.

It should be emphasized, since this essential point is obscured in previous descriptions, that in spite of the differences in the determining conditions, accent placement and word stress placement are organically related as two phases of a single process, such that accent must be assigned before word stress rules can apply. This is self-evident since linguistically functional distinctive stress has priority over non-distinctive stress. The implication that the occurrence of purely rhythmically motivated stresses can be specified in terms of the linguistic *system*, and that, in fact, it must be so specified, is of crucial importance from the point of view of this study. For we intend to show that, in principle, the alleged alternation of short and long syllables in Hungarian "quantitative" iambic verse is essentially (i.e., with the exception of the effect of an artificially superimposed prosodic convention) an alternation of unstressed and stressed or stressable syllables, and hence, by inference, *system-related*. To this extent, quantitatively defined metric rhythm is subject to linguistic description.

We can now turn to the main topic of this chapter: what conditions determine the occurrence of stresses between two accents? We have deliberately called this domain a *word*, even though it may include several words, because it appears that the entire domain functions, from the point of view of stress occurrence, *as if it were a single word*. Let us call this domain a *phonological phrase* or simply *phrase*. Consequently,

(7) the stress contour of a word and of a phrase are identical, given equal length and syllable structure.

Thus in order to describe the distribution of *all* non-distinctive stresses, it is sufficient to know the stess pattern of a single word.

Let us for convenience in the following discussion regard a *word* as a sequence of one or more syllables between a left-hand and right-hand word boundary[13] where, from left to right, each syllable is designated by an ordinal number. We can then speak of first, second, third, etc., syllable, and use the symbols S1, S2, S3, etc., respectively. Let us also assume that the word is in complete isolation, such as an item in a list (e.g. a dictionary). In this phrasing, by rule (4) primary word stress is placed on S1. Since this rule applies "invariably," primary word stress is not a function of the grammatical status, length, or phonemic structure of the word (notably, it is not affected by the length feature of S1). Furthermore, no quantitative or qualitative vowel reduction occurs in subsequent syllables as a consequence of (4).[14] The linguistic fact expressed by (4), to my knowledge, has not been challenged.[15]

There is somewhat less unanimity among previous descriptions regarding the conditions that determine the placement of secondary stress. For convenience, we can group the various proposed views into two major categories:

(A) secondary stress occurs on successive odd-numbered syllables following S1.

(B) A) is true only where odd-numbered syllables are not short; otherwise secondary stress occurs on the following (even-numbered) syllables.

Alternative (A): *position-determined stress placement*

In general, this view implies stress distribution on a strictly numerical-positional basis, irrespective of syllable length. The fact that there *is* secondary word stress in Hungarian at all was first stated explicitly by László Arany in the late nineteenth century in his study on native verse.[16] Arany noted that in longer polysyllabic words S5 receives a light stress (as in [8]) but, in words of six syllables or longer, there is no stress on S3 or S4 (9):

(8) sérenče:tlenše:tlenšè:get   'misfortune (acc.)'
    gyönyörü:še:gè:re   'to his delight'
but not
(9) *sérenčè:tlenše:gem   'my misfortune'
    *hálhatatlànša:got   'immortality (acc.)'

Subsequent studies in Arany's tradition found that, in addition to S5, S3 as well as other odd-numbered syllables also receive secondary stress. In his book on Hungarian phonetics, Balassa formulated the principle of word stress in Hungarian as follows:

> In a word pronounced by itself, the most strongly stressed member [syllable] is the first, the second is weakest, and between the two is the third as well as all subsequent odd-numbered members, while all even-numbered members are equivalent to the second in stress value.[17]

A notable aspect of Balassa's view is that he does not regard secondary stress value to be a function of word length; there are, in other words, only two non-primary stress values—"third-rate" and "fourth-rate" with respect to primary stress (which is "first-rate"). Remarkably, he seems to think in terms of *abstract values* of stress which are constant regardless of their physical realization. In a more recent study, and one concerned specifically with rhythm in native verse, Szabedi makes a somewhat similar distinction between values and their physical correlates. He argues that

> it is not sufficient to say that stress is not absolute but relative intensity [loudness]; we must say that stress is not loudness at all but rather a *ratio* [relation] of the loudness of successive syllables of varying degrees of intensity. . .
>
> The absolute intensity of syllables comprising an unstressed sequence [i.e., phrase] is identical. It is on account of the positions they occupy in a sequence that their stress values are different.[18]

Suppose we indicate values by numbers, "1" representing the highest value. Then the stress patterns of the following examples, taken from various sources, are as marked (the value "4" will be omitted for the time being):

(10) a. boldog   'happy'
        1
     b. boldogša:g   'happiness'
        1   3
     c. boldogtalan   'unhappy'
        1   3
     d. boldogtalanša:g   'unhappiness'[19]
        1   3   3

(11)   boldogtalanša:ga   'his unhappiness'[20]
          1   3   3

(12)   legešlegmegengestelhetetlenebbeknek
          1   3   3   3   3   3   3
                                        'to the most irreconcileable ones'[21]

In these examples, secondary stress occurs on every odd-numbered syllable other than S1, and the secondary stress values are shown to be identical: the succession of the value "3", as in (12), does not account for the *phonetic* fact, observed by Hall, and others, that, from left to right, secondary stresses "diminish in intensity,"[22] as shown by Hall's example,

(13)   bizalmatlanša:ggal   'with distrust'
          1   3   4

In spite of certain differences in the interpretation of phonetic facts, and, more importantly, in theoretical views, however, the descriptions alluded to uniformly claim the validity of **(A)** above. This claim correctly expresses the *general* underlying scheme or tendency in the language to make alternate vowels prominent by stress. Schematically,

(14) ...S U S U S...

where S=stressed syllable, U=unstressed syllable.

Alternative (B): *syllable length-determined stress placement*

This alternative, a more recent modification of **(A)**, asserts, in effect, that, under certain conditions, syllable length takes precedence over numerical syllable position as the condition determining the occurrence of secondary stress. Specifically, Szinnyei holds, for example, that where S3 is short, stress occurs not on S3 but on S4 instead, unless the even-numbered syllable is word-final:[23]

(15)   aranyakat   'gold (pl. acc.)'
        1   3

(16)   kæræškedælem[24]   'commerce'
        1   3

A similar view is adopted by Lotz,[25] but without the provision excepting word-final syllables. There is, in fact, yet another subtle but significant difference between these two views:

> *Szinnyei:* In längeren Wörtern fällt ausserdem ein Nebenton auf die dritte und fünfte oder (wenn *die dritte* kurz ist) auf die vierte und sechste Silbe, aber nie auf die letzte.[26]

> *Lotz:* Sehr schwacher Druck fällt auf die dritte, fünfte, u.s.w. Silbe, bzw. wenn *diese* kurz sind, auf die vierte, sechste, u.s.w. Silbe.[27]

The portions that I have in italics imply two different claims: Szinnyei would stress S4, S6, etc., if *only* S3 is short; Lotz requires that S3 and *all* following odd-numbered syllables be short in order for stress to occur on the following even-numbered syllables.

Furthermore, there is a significant omission in both of these accounts, namely, that of a specification of the length feature of the *even-numbered* syllables which are supposed to be stressed in case S3 or all odd-numbered syllables (other than S1) are short. Given one of these conditions, does stress occur on S4, S6, etc., regardless of whether they are long or short? The example (16) is not particularly revealing, nor are, in fact, other words five syllables long or shorter, since in such words the conditioning factor underlying the stress shift from S3 to S4 may be obscured by the effect of other conditions, to be discussed below. But in the light of other data, it appears fairly certain that the authors had in mind *long* even-numbered syllables as an additional condition for the proposed stress patterns. Thus, in my speech at least, secondary stress on S4 in seven-syllabics such as *alakulataikat* 'their military companies (acc.)' and *felekezeteiket* 'their religious sects (acc.)', where S3 is short but so is S4, is possible but less preferred than stress on S3, whereas *šemlegeši:thetetlen*
                                                                        1   3   3
'un-neutralizeable' is clearly a more satisfactory stress pattern than *šemlegeši:t-*
                                                                        1   3
hetetlen. Longer words serve as more convincing examples; in *megséntše:g-*
        3   3
teleni:thetetlenše:ge 'his unblasphemeableness', stress on short S5 rather than on long S6 would be considered deviant.

Although judgments of this sort are necessarily subjective and subject to idiolectal variation, there is sufficient reason to believe that the chief, and perhaps only, motivation for proposing (B) at all is to give expression to the strong potential prominence-signalling tendency of syllable length in the language. This tendency actually may not be language-specific at all. Lieberman points out that in a language where primary word stress is always on S1, the listener could

> interpret all other perceived durations (which might sometimes reflect the intensity of the speech signal as well as the duration of the segment) as manifestations of the feature *length*.[28]

Some electromyographic and psycholinguistic evidence reported by Fónagy[29] also seems to point to the tendency of length to be perceived as stress in Hungarian. Thus in addition to the principle that alternate syllables tend to be prominent by stress in Hungarian, the alternative (B), so interpreted, correctly captures a second fundamental tendency in the language, the attraction of (non-distinctive) stress by long syllables.

Even though both of these alternative views of Hungarian secondary stress incorporate some essential truths about the language, the question still needs to be asked, however, whether both can be equally correct. On logical grounds alone, they are mutually exclusive: if it *is* the case that odd-numbered syllables are (invariably) stressed, then (B) is false; if it *is* the case that there are conditions under which stress can occur on even-numbered syllables, then (A) is false.

Furthermore, it is easy to think of a great number of counterexamples against both (A) and (B). Note that both views imply, somewhat bluntly, that under such and such conditions stress is placed in such and such positions *uniquely*. Free variation, then, is excluded. Yet it is not true that in isolated words the positions of secondary stress are necessarily unique in one way or another; there is room for free variation, its range apparently increasing in proportion to word length. In many instances, the existence of two or more equally correct alternative stress contours for a word is the result of an interaction of syllable position and syllable length. For example, in (10d) and (16), each of which is supposed to be evidence in support of the view that it exemplifies and where S3 is short and S4 is long, the stress contours are completely interchangeable: *boldogtalanša:g* and *kæræškedælem* are no less
$$\text{1} \qquad \text{3} \qquad\qquad \text{1} \quad \text{3} \quad \text{3}$$
correct (cf. Table III). Nor would either of the alternative descriptions (A) and (B) account for a whole range of other possibilities including such forms as *akarat, a:rada:š, lakodalom, semtelenše:g, čoda:lkoza:š, kiaha:la:ša. bara:t-*
$$\text{1} \quad\quad \text{1} \quad\quad\quad \text{1} \quad\quad \text{3} \quad\quad \text{1} \quad\quad\quad \text{3} \quad\quad\quad \text{1} \quad \text{3} \quad\quad \text{1} \quad \text{3} \quad\quad\quad \text{1}$$
ša:ga:e:rt (cf. Tables I-III). A description of word stress in terms of conditions
$$\text{3}$$
existing *within* the word cannot account for these stress contours.

The relevant domain of secondary stress placement in Hungarian is the phonological phrase (p. 36). By (7), the stress contours of a phrase and of a word (of equal length and syllable structure) are identical, and hence the distribution of stress within a single word should reflect the stress pattern of a comparable phrase. But, by definition, a phrase occurs in a *context;* on the other hand, the stress pattern of a word in isolation does not reflect,[30] in Hungarian unlike in certain other languages such as English, the stress pattern of the same word in a phonological context. It follows that a consideration of extra-contextual word stress is not sufficient for a description of phrase stress in the language. Accordingly, next we will consider the effect of a following context on the distribution of stress within a phrasally-defined word.

Alternative (C): *context-determined stress placement.*

There are at least two general constraints on stress occurrence in Hungarian:

(17) no stressed syllable of a multisyllabic phrase may be adjacent to another stressed syllable.[31]

(18) no more than two unstressed syllables may occur in a sequence; of three such syllables the second is always stressed.[32]

(17) implies that two adjacent syllables may not be stressed either within a phrase or across an intervening phrase boundary. Since, by definition, every accented syllable represents a phrase boundary, the domain of a phrase extends from (i.e., including) an accented syllable to the syllable immediately preceding (i.e., excluding) the next accented syllable. By this principle, two stressed syllables may occur in a sequence only if both are accented, and hence signal the beginning of a phrase, but the domain of the first phrase is a single syllable. In (5′) and (19), # marks phrase boundaries:

(5′) #fégyelmezetlen#gyèrek#   'naughty child'

(19) #fégyelmezetlen a#gyèrek#   'the child is naughty'

It will be observed that, by (17), S5 in (5′) cannot have stress since it occurs next to a stressed (accented) syllable; the same holds for S2. In (19) the first phrase includes the definite article *a* (even though it is part of the following constituent) which, by (17), is unstressed, but the stress value of S5 is indeterminate. On the other hand, by (18), the first phrase in both (5′) and (19) must have at least one secondary stress; in the former, (17) permits only one, but in the latter there may be one or two.

Note, incidentally, that both of the alternatives (A) and (B) discussed above are consistent with the principles (17) and (18), although (17) is only vacuously true of a word in isolation. However, should we wish to assign secondary phrasal word stress on the basis of previous descriptions of "word stress," by applying (A) we should place stress on S5 (and S3) in (5′), and by (B), stress would fall on S4 in (19) in which case, due to (17), S5 would be (obligatorily) unstressed. The first of these is impossible and the second, as will be shown, is only one of two possible alternatives.

The foregoing considerations lead to a hypothesis that may be formulated as follows: secondary phrase stress in Hungarian is distributed, within the limitations imposed by (17) and (18), on the basis of the speaker's (subconscious) anticipation of the stress conditions in the immediately following context. It seems that at certain points in the course of speech, possibly at the beginning of each phrase, the speaker "sizes up" the distance to the next accented syllable (and hence the length of, i.e., the number of syllables in, the phrase), and once he anticipates the position of the next accent, he can *automatically calculate* the distribution of the preceding lesser stresses. The range of possible stress configurations allowed by (17) and (18) appears to be further restricted by the prominence potential of length, as already noted.

It must be pointed out that an "automatic" calculation by the speaker of the positions of stress does not imply the uniqueness of the resulting stress contour. In many instances, apparently several factors interact—notably those represented by (A), (B), and (C)—and as a result several alternative stress contours are possible which may be either free variants or represent subtle differences on a scale of acceptability.[33] Consequently, it is not being asserted here that stress patterns not accounted for by the rule proposed under (C) are necessarily deviant and violate a native speaker's intuitive sense of correctness; my main concern is to show that those patterns accounted for *are* correct, although perhaps not uniquely so.

In the remainder of this chapter, the hypothesis (C) will be tested, within the limits necessitated by the scope of this study, in terms of the syllable structures presented in Tables I-V below. The controlled variables are word length (within the range from three-syllable to seven-syllable words) and syllable length (in longer words S1 and S2 are disregarded in order to avoid unnecessary multiplication). "o" and "−" mark short and long syllables, respectively. All the illustrative examples are from Standard Hungarian; prefixed forms and compounds have been avoided[34] where possible.

TABLE I

Three-syllabics

	S1	S2	S3		
(a)		o	o	akarat, ba:natoš	'will', 'sad'
(b)		o	−	savaza:š, a:rada:š	'voting', 'flood'
(c)		−	o	bara:tom, a:lda:šok	'my friend', 'blessings'
(d)		−	−	kere:kne:l, boldogša:g	'at a wheel', 'happiness'

TABLE II

Four-syllabics

	S1	S2	S3	S4			
(a)	o	o	o	o	lakodalom, ba:mulata	'wedding party',	'his amazement'
(b)	o	o	o	—	felešele:š, va:rakozo:	'talking back',	'waiting'
(c)	o	o	—	o	vesedelmeš, e:rvele:še	'dangerous',	'his argument'
(d)	o	o	—	—	pohara:bo:l, semtelenše:g	'from its glass',	'impertinence'
(e)	—	—	o	o	šebe:seten, sa:nde:košan	'on surgery',	'intentionally'
(f)	—	—	o	—	čoda:lkoza:š, hatytyu:ito:l	'being surprised',	'from its swans'
(g)	—	—	—	o	vese:je:re, kendö:je:be	'to its danger',	'into its scarf'
(h)	—	—	—	—	tulajdonša:g, fe:le:nkše:ge:t	'characteristic',	'its fright(acc.)'

TABLE III

Five-syllabics

	S1	S2	S3	S4	S5		
(a)	o	o	o	o	o	felekezetem, sa:zadainak	'my sect', 'to its company'
(b)	o	o	o	o	–	feleleteink, rettenetešebb	'our answers', 'more terrible'
(c)	o	o	o	–	o	saporoda:ša, nemzetiše:gi	'its multiplication', 'of nationality'
(d)	o	o	o	–	–	maradiša:ga:t, la:togata:še:rt	'his conservatism', 'for a visit'
(e)	o	o	–	o	o	tudoma:nyošan, közleme:nyeik	'scientifically', 'their announcements'
(f)	o	o	–	o	–	magyara:zata:t, kezdeme:nyeze:š	'his explanation(acc.)', 'initiation'
(g)	o	o	–	–	o	kiaba:la:ša, telješi:tme:nyek	'his shouting', 'accomplishments'
(h)	o	o	–	–	–	egyenetlenše:g, o:vatošša:gbo:l	'unevenness', 'as a precaution'
(i)	o	–	o	o	o	tana:čtalanok, sa:nde:kainak	'helpless(pl.)', 'of its intentions'
(j)	o	–	o	o	–	töke:leteši:t, e:rve:nyešüle:š	'he perfects', 'success'
(k)	o	–	o	–	o	fegyelmezetlen, po:tolhatatlan	'undisciplined', 'irreplaceable'
(l)	o	–	o	–	–	višelkede:še:t, emle:kezetbö:l	'his behavior(acc.)', 'from memory'
(m)	o	–	–	o	o	kisa:mi:thatom, ingerle:kenyek	'I may figure out', 'irritable(pl.)'
(n)	o	–	–	o	–	elengedhetö: išme:telhetö:	'excusable', 'repeatable'
(o)	o	–	–	–	o	makačša:ga:nak, arca:tlanša:ga:t	'of its stubbornness', 'its impudence(acc.)'
(p)	o	–	–	–	–	bara:tša:ga:e:rt, függetlenše:ge:n	'for his friendship', 'on its independence'

TABLE IV

Six-syllabics

	S1	S2	S3	S4	S5	S6		
(a)	o	o	o	o	o	o	kerületeitek, következetešen	'your districts', 'consistently'
(b)	o	o	o	o	o	—	feleleteike:rt, tapastalataink	'for their answers', 'our experiences'
(c)	o	o	o	o	—	o	a:llhatatošabban, nyilatkozatukkal	'more steadfastly', 'with their comment'
(d)	o	o	o	o	—	—	kerešeteikbö:l, kiše:releteze:štö:l	'from their salaries', 'from experimenting'
(e)	o	o	o	—	o	o	va:rakoza:šokat, ke:rlelhetetlenül	'expectations(acc.)', 'implacably'
(f)	o	o	o	—	o	—	anyagiašdoda:š, e:rintkeze:šeink	'money-mindedness', 'our contacts'
(g)	o	o	o	—	—	o	saporoda:ša:nak, magyartalanša:gok	'of its multiplication', 'un-Hungarianisms'
(h)	o	o	o	—	—	—	ve:glegeši:tette:k, következetlenše:g	'they finalized it', 'inconsistency'
(i)	o	o	—	o	o	o	e:rtekezleteken, bolondša:gaival	'at meetings', 'with his foolishness(pl.)'
(j)	o	o	—	o	o	—	fa:radalmaime:rt, fordi:ta:šaibo:l	'for my efforts', 'from its translations'
(k)	o	o	—	o	—	o	servezetlenebben, minö:ši:thetetlen	'more disorganized', 'unqualifiable'
(l)	o	o	—	o	—	—	fojtato:lagošša:g, eredme:nytelenše:g	'continuity', 'failure'
(m)	o	o	—	—	o	o	sellemešše:geket, isme:tlö:de:šeit	'wittiness(pl.)', 'its repetitions(acc.)'
(n)	o	o	—	—	o	—	ellenö:rizhetö:, ellenše:geškede:š	'checkable', 'hostility'
(o)	o	o	—	—	—	o	halhatatlanša:ga, va:laste:košša:ga	'its immortality', 'its exquisitness'
(p)	o	o	—	—	—	—	ke:sületlenše:ge:t, seme:rmetlenše:gbö:l	'its unpreparedness(acc.)', 'out of impudence'

TABLE V/A

Seven-syllabics

	S1	S2	S3	S4	S5	S6	S7		
(a)			o	o	o	o	o	alakulataikat	'their companies(acc.)'
(b)			o	o	o	o	—	alakulataike:rt	'for their companies'
(c)			o	o	—	o	o	a:llhatatošabbjaik	'their more steadfast ones'
(d)			o	o	—	o	—	lendületešebbeke:rt	'for more energetic ones'
(e)			o	—	o	o	o	saporoda:šaira	'to their multiplication'
(f)			o	—	o	o	—	kavaroda:šaito:l	'from its confusion'
(g)			o	—	—	o	o	me:rte:ktelenše:geken	'on extravagance(pl.)'
(h)			o	—	—	o	—	a:llamoši:ta:šokon	'on nationalization(pl.)'
(i)			—	o	o	o	o	a:ldoma:šaitokat	'your toasts (by drink)'
(j)			—	o	o	o	—	sövetše:gešeitö:l	'from its allies'
(k)			—	o	—	o	o	felede:kenyebbjei	'its more forgetful ones'
(l)			—	o	—	o	—	kalandozgata:šaink	'our adventures'
(m)			—	—	o	o	o	nyomoru:ša:gaira	'on its miseries'
(n)			—	—	o	o	—	alapi:tva:nyaibo:l	'from its foundations'
(o)			—	—	—	o	o	serenče:tlenše:geken	'on misfortunes'
(p)			—	—	—	o	—	tervserü:tlenše:geink	'our unsystematicalness'

TABLE V/B

Seven-syllabics

	S1	S2	S3	S4	S5	S6	S7		
(a)			o	o	o	—	o	felekezeteikre	'to their sects'
(b)			o	o	o	—	—	fiatalosoda:sa:t	'its juvenation' (its becoming young(acc.))
(c)			o	o	—	—	o	eredetise:ge:vel	'with its originality'
(d)			o	o	—	—	—	demokratikussa:ga:t	'its democraticalness(acc.)'
(e)			o	—	o	—	o	semlegesi:thetetlen	'un-neutralizable'
(f)			o	—	o	—	—	civiliza:cio:ja:t	'its civilization(acc.)'
(g)			o	—	—	—	o	villamosi:ta:sa:ra	'on its electrification'
(h)			o	—	—	—	—	felesslegesse:ge:ro:l	'from its superfluity'
(i)			—	o	o	—	o	va:sa:rla:saitokkal	'with your shoppings'
(j)			—	o	o	—	—	eredme:nytelenebbe:	'more unsuccessful(inch.)'
(k)			—	o	—	—	o	vira:goztata:sa:ra	'for its flowering'
(l)			—	o	—	—	—	fojtato:lagossa:ga:t	'its continuity(acc.)'
(m)			—	—	o	—	o	gyümölcöztethetetlen	'sterile'
(n)			—	—	o	—	—	esetlense:geikto:l	'from their clumsiness(pl.)'
(o)			—	—	—	—	o	e:rtelmetlense:ge:nek	'of its senselessness'
(p)			—	—	—	—	—	halhatatlansa:ga:ro:l	'from its immortality'

A phrasal word may appear in one of three contexts:

(20) _____X́

(21) _____XX́

(22) _____##

where X is any syllable, ´ is accent, and ## is sentence boundary. (20) and (21) are equivalent to the respective contexts of the word *fegyelmezetlen* in (5′) and (19). We assume, in other words, that the unstressed syllable X—obligatorily unstressed by (17)—belongs to the context, even though, properly speaking, it is included in the preceding phrase. Actually, the word *fegyelmezetlen* AND its context *a*, which together comprise a phrase in (19), are identical in syllable structure to the single word *fegyelmezetlenül* 'naughtily', for example, and hence represent the same domain of stress placement. Thus a three-syllabic word in (20) is equivalent, so far as stress assignment is concerned, to a two-syllabic in (21); a four-syllabic in (20) is equivalent to a three-syllabic in (21); etc. In general, an *n*—syllabic in (20) is equivalent to an *n*−1 syllabic in (21).

Given (20) and (21), let us call the accented syllable X́, and from right to left, the successively preceding syllables X́−1, X́−2, etc., (read: X minus one). Then, for any phrasal word in either context, stress distribution may be determined as follows:

Starting with X́ and moving from right to left, X́−1 is invariably unstressed, by (17). Next X́−2 is examined which may be long or short; if long, it receives stress, and if short, it may receive stress. However, in case X́−2 is assigned no stress, then by (18), X́−3 must be stressed (regardless of syllable structure).

This principle may be expressed in the form of a set of somewhat simplified rules such as (23). The rules apply to any phonological phrase whose right-hand boundary is not a sentence boundary (cf. [22]).

(23) (1) X ⟶ [stress] / X _____ X # X́
                              [long]

(2) X ⟶ [stress] / X _____ X # X́
                          [short]

(3) X ⟶ [stress] / X _____[short] X # X́

The rules (23) assert, then, that in a phrasal word immediately followed by an accented syllable stress is obligatory on the penultimate syllable if long, optional on the penultimate syllable if short, and obligatory on the ante-penultimate syllable irrespective of the length feature. Note, however, that in a given instance only one of the three rules can apply, and then only if the preceding rules have not applied. (23.1-3) are thus disjunctively ordered with respect to one another: once (23.1) has applied, the rest cannot apply; once (23.2) has applied, (23.3) cannot apply; but if neither (23.1) nor (23.2) has been applied, (23.3) must be applied. The principle of ordering enables us to express these relationships in a simpler manner: since any syllable to which (23.1) does not apply must be short, the specification [short] in the rules can be eliminated, i.e., in (23.3) replaced by an optional syllable of unspecified length. By collapsing (23. 1-3) into a single rule, we obtain (23′):

$$(23′) \quad X \longrightarrow \quad [\text{stress}] \quad / \quad X \left\{ \begin{array}{l} (a)\underline{\qquad} \\ \text{long} \\ (b)\underline{\qquad}(X) \end{array} \right\} \quad X \# \acute{X}$$

Let us for the moment mark secondary stresses assigned by the rule (23′) by ˇ . Then, in view of (23′), in the context (20) (i.e., ____Ẋ), for all forms in Table V/B (henceforth V/B), Ṡ6, and for all those in V/A, optionally Ṡ6~Ṡ5. Similarly, for IV c, d, g, h, k, l, o, p, Ṡ5, and for the rest Ṡ5~Ṡ4; for III c, d, g, h, k, l, o, p, Ṡ4, and for the rest Ṡ4~Ṡ3; for II c, d, g, h, Ṡ3, but if, for II a, b, e, f, the second option is taken, then (17) is violated; the same is true of all items in I. On the other hand, in the context (21) (i.e., ____ XẊ), for all long S7's in V/A and V/B, Ṡ7, and for all short S7's, Ṡ7~Ṡ6; for all long S6's in IV, Ṡ6, and for all short S6's, Ṡ6~Ṡ5; for all long S5's in III, Ṡ5, and for all short S5's, Ṡ5~Ṡ4; for all long S4's in II, Ṡ4, and for all short S4's, Ṡ4~Ṡ3; for long S3's in I, Ṡ3, but again the second option for short S3's would violate (17).

Although (23′) accounts for the general principle that syllable length is a strong conditioning factor in secondary stress placement, and also expresses the principle of syllable alternation discussed under (A), it violates (17) in shorter words and (18) in longer words. Specifically, in order to obtain only correct stress contours, (23′) must be blocked where it would assign stress to an S2, and its applicability must be extended so that no more than two unstressed syllables occur in a sequence.

In order to eliminate the first problem we shall reintroduce the rule (4), which places stress on S1, as the rule (24). That there is already stress in the form of accent on S1 need cause no difficulty. The positions of accent within a sentence designate the boundaries of the domain—the phonological phrase—to which (23′) applies. In this sense, then, accent has a demarcative function.[35] Once various degrees of accent have been distributed on grammatical-semantic grounds, positions of accent are not subject to change by subsequent stress placement rules. But it is possible to *reassign* stress to an accented syllable; note that such a syllable may carry a stronger or weaker accent with respect to other accented syllables, but the stress which (24) reassigns to it will always be the strongest (i.e., primary) with respect to other stresses within the phonological phrase to which it belongs.

(24) $X \longrightarrow$ [stress] / #_____

Let us require that (24) and (23') apply *in this order*; then, once primary stress has been placed on S1 by (24), S2 cannot be assigned stress by a subsequent application of (23'). A single application of (24), and the consequent inapplicability of (23'), assure that the correct stress configuration will occur in phrasal words up to three syllables long.

Obviously, the amount of data accounted for by this procedure is very limited. There is no reason to suppose, however, that the principle of stress placement which operates in short words or phrases does not equally account for the distribution of stress in longer syllable sequences. Note again that what this principle asserts is that in estimating the arrangement of lesser stresses within a (phrasal) word, after stressing S1, the speaker uses as his point of reference the *next* accented (or stressed) syllable, rather than the preceding one. Thus the mental process which we attempt to express by the rules (24) and (23') may be assumed to operate in a *cyclic* manner in a right to left direction,[36] regardless of the number of syllables included within the domain in which it applies, until the rules become inapplicable and the distribution of stresses is complete. The phrasal word stress rule (25), then, differs from (23') in that the rightmost X in the context may now be *any* stressed (i.e., not only an accented) syllable, and the righthand phrase boundary will now be optional:

(25) $X \longrightarrow$ [stress] / X $\left\{ \begin{array}{l} \text{(a)} \overline{\text{[long]}} \\ \text{(b)} \underline{\quad\quad} \text{(X)} \end{array} \right\}$ X (#) X́

Let us again suppose that (24) and (25) apply in this order. Furthermore, let us follow the convention that (24) assigns the stress value "1" (to the S1 of the domain), and every time (25) is applied, it assigns the stress value "2". After each application of (25), all previously assigned stresses *other than "1"* will be reduced by one. By special convention, after the final rule application all stress values other than "1" are in addition further reduced by one.[37]

We can now briefly return to the problem left unsolved on page 50. (23') was found applicable, by implication, from seven-syllables down to the forms II e, d, g, h in (20). Now the second option for II a, b, e, f does not exist due to (25b), and hence stress must occur on S3; (24) places stress on S1. The same holds for short S3's of I in (21).

The following examples illustrate the applicability of (24) and (25). Following the initial application of (24), only (25) is applicable within a given domain. Each line of numbers (except the first and last) represents one application of (25). The last syllables are assumed to have the length feature shown, i.e., the first consonantal segment of the following X is considered irrelevant here.

V/B(g)   villamoši:ta:ša:ra[38]   / _____ X́   (20)
          1   by (24)
                        2   by (25a)
                  2   3   by (25a)
                  3   4   by conv.

                                             / _____ X X́   (21)
          1   by (24)
                              2   by (25a)
                        2   3   by (25a)
                  2   3   4   by (25b)
                  3   4   5   by conv.

         or, alternatively, (24), (25b), (25a), as in (20)

IV(g)   saporoda:ša:nak   / _____ X́   (20)
          1   by (24)
                        2   by (25a)
                  2   3   by (25b)
                  3   4   by conv.

                                             / _____ X X́
          1   by (24)
                              2   by (25b)
                        2   3   by (25a)
                        3   4   by conv.

         or, alternatively, (24), (25b), (25b), as in (20)

III(j)   e:rve:nyešüle:š   / _____ X́   (20)
          1   by (24)
                        2   by (25b)
                        3   by conv.

or:

1			by (24)
	2		by (25b)
	3		by conv.

/ _____ X X́

1			by (24)
	2		by (25a)
	2	3	by (25b)
	3	4	by conv.

II(h)   tulajdonša:g   / _____ X́

1		by (24)
	2	by (25a)
	3	by conv.

/ _____ X X́ (21)

1		by (24)
	2	by (25a)
	3	by conv.

I(a)   akarat   / _____ X́ (20)

1	by (24)

/ _____ X X́ (21)

1		by (24)
	2	by (25b)
	3	by conv.

The principle of context-determined stress placement which has been outlined here accounts for a number of significant facts that earlier descriptions correctly observed, and it also clarifies some issues that have remained blurred or have been left without an adequate explanation. The rule (25) incorporates the general constraints (17) and (18), and correctly assigns the stress patterns in the illustrative examples previously cited (10, 11, 13, 15, 16, etc.). Note, however, that in order to obtain these stress patterns we are forced to assume each of the 'odd-syllabic' words to be in (20), and to further assume that, except in (16), the optional context in (25 b) is not applicable. If we fail to make these assumptions, then by applying (25) we obtain the following stress configurations as well:

(10b′) boldogša:g
        1

(10c′) boldogtalan
        1   3

(10d′) boldogtalanša:g
        1   3

(15′)   aranyakat
       1   3

(16′)   kæræškedælem
      1   3   4

all of which, in my speech, are equally acceptable stress patterns of the words when the latter are pronounced in isolation.[39] This lends further support to the contention that there is no "word stress" in Hungarian, insofar as the term designates the unique assignability of a stress contour to a word in isolation. Given a transformational-generative framework of reference, all lexical elements are listed in the lexicon without any stress being marked; syntactic outputs are assigned accents over limited domains by rules such as (1) and (2) and in accordance with (4), and further stress distinctions are made on the basis of the principles expressed by (25). Thus it appears that the stress contour of a word out of context is derived through the speaker's subconscious association of the word with, or his anticipation of, one of the following contexts so far discussed. This phenomenon needs further study.

    Furthermore, the rule (25) gives expression to the characteristic rhythmic tendency in the language represented by (14) above which serves as the basis for both of the alternative descriptions (A) and (B), and incorporates the provision allowing for the occurrence of the stress configuration (14′) in (B):

(14′) ...S U U S...

It is crucial to point out, however, that, unlike previous descriptions, (25) accounts for the possibility of the pattern (14′) *regardless of the length feature* of the second of two consecutive unstressed syllables. It will be recalled that

(14′) is excluded by the alternative (A) altogether, and (B) requires that the second U be short. By (25), however, phrasal words having the structure of III e-h, m-p, IV i-p, V i-p (see tables) can be assigned stress on S3; nor is it in fact rendered obligatory by (25), unlike by (B), for S4 to have the strongest secondary stress in case S3 is short. The fundamental stress pattern of Hungarian may then be schematically represented as

(26)   S   U   (S)   U   S

(where the S in parenthesis may or may not be present), and may be said to be ultimately contextually determined.

The principle of context-determined stress distribution also casts some light on Szinnyei's somewhat mysterious condition requiring an even-numbered syllable bearing secondary stress to be non-final. Perhaps one can speculate that the motivation for setting this condition is the constraint expressed in (17): if we suppose that Szinnyei's "word" corresponds to what we have labelled "phrasal word," and is therefore immediately followed by an accented S1, then this explanation is not implausible.

In view of the foregoing discussion of stress in Hungarian, we can now return to the context (22) which has so far been ignored. The rule (25) does not account for stress distribution within a (phrasal) word in the context (22). It assumes, in other words, that the right-hand context is other than zero. A phrasal word in (22) amounts to the word in isolation, and it was suggested earlier that apparently a speaker distributes stresses over such a domain as if the context were either (20) or (21). In other words, stress may or may not occur on the final syllable. Since, then, before a major boundary stress is placed as if the context were either _____## or _____X ##, the rule (25) may be modified by the addition of the context _____(X) ##:

$$(25') \qquad \qquad \ldots \quad \left\{ \begin{array}{cc} (X) & \# \# \\ X & (\#) \quad \acute{X} \end{array} \right\}$$

To what extent there is free variation among the three possible stressed positions immediately preceding a sentence boundary is a question that requires further research. It appears that in many instances the numerical principle predominates, so that successive odd-numbered syllables in the word in the context in question are stressed; thus of the phrasal words

(26)   ša:torok alatt   'under the tents'
         1   3   4

(27) va:lassunk magunknak   'let's choose for ourselves'
      1   3   4

(26) is taken to be in the context _____## and (27) in _____X ##.

It goes without saying that it would be possible to state the relevant conditions pertaining to the placement of phrase stress in Hungarian in separate rules: one expressing the numerical principle, another stating the role of syllable length, and still a third accounting for the effect of a following context. Such a listing of rules, however, would fail to express the underlying relationship among these conditions. The rule (25'), though perhaps only a rough approximation, comes closer, I believe, to representing the speaker's criteria for arranging lesser stresses between two accents, and, applied cyclically, better expresses the apparent mental processes involved than the 'static' concepts discussed in the first part of this chapter.

In anticipation of the discussion in the following chapter, a few additional remarks are in order concerning the concept of "phrase".

Earlier in this chapter we defined a phrase as a sequence of syllables between two accents (excluding the second one). Later we found that the right-hand boundary of a phrase may also be represented by the syllable immediately preceding a sentence boundary (##) rather than an accented syllable. Now it can be pointed out that the left-hand phrase boundary, which is always an accented syllable, may not always be immediately preceded by a sentence boundary, since one or more *pre-phrasal* syllables may occur between the beginning of the sentence and the first accented syllable. Pre-phrasal syllables can also be numbered[40] with respect to the first accented syllable, but also given a — ("minus") value:

$$\#\#\ldots S\text{-}3 \quad S\text{-}2 \quad S^{\pm}1 \quad S2 \quad S3 \quad S4 \ldots$$

where $S^{\pm}1$ has accent and is therefore the beginning of the first phrase. Syllables with negative positional value are assigned stress the same way as their positive counterparts, apparently in accordance with (14)[41]: hence every odd-numbered syllable gets secondary stress.

A second remark concerns the manner in which accents are distributed on a grammatical-semantic basis, and thus the boundaries of phrases are set. It is understood that, in principle, any syllable to which (4) applies may be assigned accent; emphatic or contrastive stress may, of course, occur on any syllable. In practice, the range of accentable syllables is generally restricted to S1's of "content words," while "function words" generally do not serve as phrase boundaries. We have noted, furthermore, that, barring factors such as word length, weaker accents are said to occur or not to occur often on the basis of whether or not the speaker considers the respective words semantically important.

To this extent, a description of the distribution of sentence stress is in part a semantic problem and is beyond the scope of this study. What does need to be pointed out, however, is that if, depending on the presence or absence of semantically motivated weaker accents, a grammatical phrase may either function as a single phonological phrase or be divided into several such phrases, then, regardless of semantic considerations, all the resulting phrase stress contours must have some psychological reality for a native speaker. Specifically, given a grammatical phrase such as *va:ltozo: serenče* (see line 15 in Text) with the constituent structure *adjective - noun* (cf. rule [1]), the syllable *va:l-* receives strong accent; but now I may or may not consider the noun *serenče* semantically important enough to accent it (on S1). If I do, then the grammatical phrase is divided into two phonological phrases and stress is placed as in (28); if I do not, then the entire grammatical phrase is a single phonological phrase and the stress pattern is as in (29) (´ and ` mark strong and weak accents, respectively; numbers mark phrase stress):

(28) #vá:ltozo:#sèrenče#
              3

(29) #vá:ltozo: serenče#
         3   4

The specification of under just what conditions the rule accounting for (28) applies is a purely descriptive task, although no doubt a difficult one. The point is that *both* stress contours are acceptable to a native speaker; the occurrence of (29) where the (semantic) context would require (28), or vice versa, does not interfere with intelligibility (although it might bring about cases of ambiguity), nor does it create a counter-intuitive effect: it is simply a *marked* form. Reference to stylistic markedness implies that the form is marked with respect to some unmarked form which, in the present view, it is the task of grammar proper to provide a description of. The property of markedness, then, in this sense, identifies a linguistic form as representing a particular stylistic level of usage. A central goal of this study is to show that stylistically marked forms can be described in terms of, and as extensions of, stylistically unmarked grammatical outputs. It is for this reason that I argue that the occurrence in strong metric positions of the syllables *o:-s* and *enč* (of [29]), for example, is acceptable as "natural" to a native speaker-reader no less on account of the *stressability* of these syllables than by virtue of their perceived length in relation to neighboring syllables.

A special case of the above is one involving monosyllables as first members of grammatical phrases. There appears to be a tendency in the language for a monosyllable and a following syntactically closely related word to function, so far as stress placement is concerned, as a single phrase.[42] In *nem tala:lom* 'I do not find it', for example, by (2), the negative particle receives strong accent but *ta* generally does not, due to the constraint expressed in (17); hence stress is distributed as in a single phrase: *ném tala:lom*. In other similar instances, phrasal
                                    3
stress contours are less unique (contrastive stress is being disregarded):e.g., *nem e:hezik* 'he is not starving' where the first syllable following *nem* is long and the second one is short. Here *ném e:hezik* and *ném e:hezik* appear equally
                       3   3
acceptable as phrasal stress contours, nor is, in fact, the occurrence of a certain degree of stress on *e:* unacceptable, although it is supposed to violate the constraint (17). This, again, would be a marked form; the juxtaposition in such instances of two stressed syllables may be possible because the *underlying source* of the phrase involved apparently has a strong psychological reality. This source is lexical stress: in a grammatical sequence that represents surface structure, stress on *any* S1, regardless of the distribution of semantically motivated accents of various degrees, is psychologically 'real' to a native speaker in a way stress on an S2 (following a phrase-initial S1) is not. For whatever are the processes involved, a semantically correct stress contour such as that in *ném e:hezik* is
                                                                              3
derived from the underlying lexical source *ném, é:hezik;*[43] the recognition of this fact is crucial to the study of metric language, for it is the *potential stressability* of any S1 in the language (cf. rule [4]) that enables a native reader to accept that syllable in a strong metric position, even though its prominence may not be semantically justified, rather than merely the length of the syllable in relation to neighboring syllables. For how else could necessarily short monosyllabic function words such as *ha, de,* etc., to cite extreme cases, fulfill the role of signalling metric prominence?

Prominence achieved by stressability, then, is to be distinguished from that achieved by stress, distinctive or non-distinctive. Stress is assigned through phonological processes (rules): all stressed syllables are included in the set of stressable syllables, but not all stressable syllables are necessarily assigned stress. The following chapter will attempt to demonstrate that stressable but ordinarily unstressed syllables occupying strong metric positions can be assigned *metrically marked* stress by the stress placement rule formulated in the present chapter.

NOTES

1. 1956, p. 24.

2. For recent generative discussions of Hungarian segmental phonology, see Rice 1965, 1967, and Szépe 1967. Among previous treatments the two best known outside of Hungary are Hall 1944 and Lotz 1939.

3. Rhythm amounts to a regularly recurrent breaking of monotony; rhythm in speech is brought about by a periodic alternation of more prominent and less prominent syllables. For a discussion of the notion of linguistic prominence in the light of recent psycho-acoustic research, see Lieberman 1967. Classe's treatment of English prose rhythm (1939) anticipates several more recent linguistic insights into the nature of stress and its bearing on rhythm. For a comprehensive discussion on some abstract properties of rhythm and for references, see Chatman 1965, pp. 18-29.

4. For example, Horváth 1951, p. 18; Vargyas 1952, p. 194.

5. The view of language and the framework of reference adhered to in this study are in general consistent with transformational theory; see Chomsky 1965, pp. 3-62, and references there. The basis for the treatment of stress given here is that of generative phonology; see especially Chomsky and Halle 1968.

6. See Tompa 1962, p. 468. It is possible that the relevant conditioning factor is the length of the modified member rather than that of the entire construction. This question needs further study. At any rate, Tompa correctly observes that "in this and similar cases, the relationship between stress distribution and rhythmic tendencies is undeniable."

7. Tompa 1962, p. 460. Elsewhere (p. 461) a paraphrased version of the same passage is called "the principal law of stress distribution."

8. 1887, p. 408. In principle, this criterion is true for any language and is thus not language specific. The question is, of course, whether there is any

systematic correlation between the speaker's judgment of semantic importance and his choice of the syntactic patterns whereby the meaning is expressed. Although this problem in Hungarian has been studied so little that at the moment almost nothing can be said about it with certainty, one might speculate that many of the differences in 'semantic importance' involve subtle subcategorial distinctions among constituents, and are therefore predictable. The rules (1) and (2) above are no doubt oversimplified and subject to refinement, but they do provide a basis for illustrating the general principles with which this chapter is concerned.

9. pp. 408-12.

10. Balassa's treatment is essentially followed in more recent grammars such as Klemm 1928 and Tompa 1961, 1962. In his study of constructive features in Hungarian, Juhasz notes that Balassa's statements on Hungarian stress "hold up well under the most scrutinous examination" (1961, p. 10).

11. The main difficulty in analyzing Balassa's examples lies in the manner in which he selected them: he took all of his illustrative material from a single play (comedy), i.e., from a context (and a specific level of style). Balassa mistakenly assumes that a form will necessarily have the same stress pattern in isolation as in a context. Other difficulties are noted by Gombócz in his review (1904) of Balassa 1904 which includes much of the material contained in his 1887 paper.

12. Cf. rule (1). See Tompa 1962, p. 461. Cf. Bánhidi et. al., 1965, p. 61.

13. This definition of the word is obviously circular. However, the grammar (which stress description is assumed to be based on, in part) provides information on word boundaries (as well as constituent membership and phonemic structure). In generative transformational terms, the stress rules given below operate on syntactic surface structures which contain all the above information.

14. One plausible explanation for the lack of vowel reduction in Hungarian is the relative phonetic weakness of strong stress, as compared to English or German.

15. In most Finno-Ugric languages stress distribution appears to be similar to that in Hungarian (Balassa 1904, p. 147; Collinder 1965, pp. 41-43).

Furthermore, it seems that at least for the last two thousand years (word) stress conditions in Hungarian have remained unchanged (Bárczi 1963, p. 54).

16. 1898. Arany's study was the first to suggest a basic relationship between prose rhythm and native verse rhythm in the light of stress occurrence.

17. 1904, p. 145.

18. 1955, pp. 109-110.

19. Sauvageot 1951, p. 25.

20. Gombócz n.d., #53.

21. Bárczi 1960, p. 33.

22. 1944, p. 17.

23. 1912, p. 12.

24. Szinnyei's spelling is given in a slightly modified form. $/\text{æ}/$ is a low front vowel which is no longer in phonemic contrast with $/\varepsilon/$. The $/\text{æ} \sim \varepsilon/$ variation is of substantial historical and descriptive significance. For a recent study of the status of $/\text{æ} \sim \varepsilon/$ in the Budapest dialect, see G. Varga 1968, pp. 19-33, and references given there.

25. 1939, p. 36.

26. p. 12.

27. p. 36.

28. 1967, p. 31.

29. 1959, pp. 24-72. Also see references given there.

30. Not necessarily, in any case, except for primary stress on S1. The few exceptions in English include such variations as stress on the first or the second syllable in *almost*, the position of stress apparently depending on whether or not the following syllable is stressed.

31. This principle, apparently not explicitly formulated before, is a logical extension of the well-known constraint that S2 is never stressed. As noted elsewhere in this book, (17) supposes normal, continuous pronunciation; that in actual speech ('performance') pauses often occur within phonological phrases and as a result the syllable following the pause receives a certain degree of stress does not affect this principle, since phrase boundaries, unlike such internal pauses, are formally defined within the grammar.

32. This principle may well express a physiological constraint, and is in that case universally valid.

33. Cf. Chomsky 1965, p. 11. The exact conditions that determine degrees of acceptability in this case are not known and require further investigation. Some stress configurations 'sound better' to a native speaker than others, but even in such judgements disagreements among speakers do occur. The conclusions of this chapter notwithstanding, the exact clues to which a speaker responds in producing particular stress contours remains an unsettled issue. Unless noted otherwise, the data presented here reflect my own speech and may not be endorsed in every detail by some other native speaker of the language.

34. Because in many such forms the positions of stress are unstable. For example, in prefixed verbs primary stress often shifts from the (monosyllabic) prefix to the verb stem, as in *meg-ö:rülök* 'I'll go mad', although academicians consider such occurrences impermissible (Tompa 1962, p. 469). In compounds, stress often occurs on the S1 of the second member, apparently depending on such factors as the length of the component words, the recency of the compound, and the part of speech status of the constituent members.

35. The notion of the demarcative function of positionally fixed stress was first proposed by Troubetzkoj. For references and discussion, see Laziczius 1944.

36. The concept of the transformational cycle is proposed in Chomsky and Halle 1968. The authors note that "the transformational cycle might apply vacuously in a certain language, in particular, if the language has very shallow surface structure. Thus a highly agglutinative language might be expected to offer little or no support for the principle of the transformational cycle, at least within the bounds of a word" (p. 25). Hungarian could be a case in point; it seems, however, that the cyclic principle does operate non-vacuously in the

language, even though the present utilization of the principle differs from its application to English by Chomsky and Halle in at least two important respects: first, primary word stress in Hungarian is assigned at the very ·beginning of the cyclic process, and thus, unlike in English, not in relation to stresses previously placed by the same rule; secondly, in Hungarian the domain to which the word stress rule applies is not syntactically defined (i.e., does not contain hierarchic constituent markers).

37. For the mechanics of this procedure, see Parts I-II, Chomsky and Halle 1968.

38. In some idiolects *villamoši:ta:ša:ra* may be equally acceptable. It may
$$\underset{1\quad3\quad4}{}$$
prove necessary that (25) be adjusted so that it provides an option for stress on X-3 (if long), in case X-2 is long. As already noted, the longer the word the more free variation is to be expected, and hence the fewer constraints the rule may contain.

39. The same does not appear to be the case with (1) and (13), both six-syllabics, and the somewhat monstrous example (12). Thus in the first two cases I find secondary stress on S4 unacceptable. It is not clear whether word length, the length feature of certain syllables (short S6, for example), or some other factor is involved here.

40. As suggested by Balassa (1904, p. 145).

41. However, S-4, for example, in the context ##_____ is generally stressed, e.g., *ha majd a korma:ny* 'when the government'. This phenomenon
$$\underset{\quad3\qquad\quad1}{}$$
may be due to the strong tendency of 'first' syllables to be stressed in Hungarian: other things equal (e.g., given a succession of unaccented and semantically negligible function words as above), the syllable immediately following a pause and thus breaking the silence is likely to be pronounced with more force than the rest. Phonetic studies in Hungarian have shown that a linguistically unstressed syllable such as an article is often pronounced louder at the beginning of a sentence than *any* syllable in the rest of the sentence (Fónagy 1958, pp. 130-1. Also cf. Horváth 1948, p. 148).

42. See Balassa 1904, p. 145; Klemm 1928, p. 627 and references given there. A similar observation by Collinder (1937, p. 112) is disputed by Fónagy (1958, p. 65). Collinder claims that in the expression *ennek egy hala:l nem ele:g*

'for him one death is not enough', stress occurs not on the S1 but on the S2 of the words *hala:l* and *ele:g*. Considering that these words belong to the respective phonological phrases *egy hala:l* and *nem ele:g*, the assertion that stress falls on
$$1 \qquad\qquad 1$$
the respective S3's is not entirely without foundation. But in the first example at least such stress may be prevented by the following stressed syllable.

43. It is interesting to note the manner in which this fundamental fact is pointed out by Klemm by means of an example: *"mind - élvitte:k ⟶ mind elvitte:k"* 'they took them all' (1928, p. 827). Klemm does not indicate secondary word stresses but notes that the two words "merge" into a single "section".

IV
ANALYSIS

The purpose of this chapter is to test the hypothesis formulated in the first part of the book: users of the language utilize the same rhythmic principles in verse as in ordinary discourse, and we ought to be able to demonstrate this fundamental relationship. Specifically, it has been proposed that the regular alternation of short and long time-units which defines the abstract metric frame is linguistically manifested by an alternation of syllables that may be long or short but are generally stressed or stressable. This argument can be supported by two important facts: first, stress is both a necessary and a sufficient condition for some syllables to be metrically prominent; secondly, regular short-long syllable alternation throughout a line, which ideally is a necessary condition for the metric rhythm to be realized by quantitative means, is relatively rare, and in its absence admittedly stress alternation assumes its function. Furthermore, it has been noted that the quantitative concept requires a non-linguistic, system-independent definition of 'syllable' and 'prominence', and hence it provides no basis for a specification of the rhythmic behavior of sentences in the metric framework in terms of the grammar, and ultimately in relation to the linguistic knowledge of speakers and listeners. We have suggested that this behavior can be partially accounted for by examining the relationship between the rules of quantitative prosody and the distribution of word stress in the language; we have speculated that syllable length could become a successful metric principle primarily by virtue of its phonetic relationship to stress and its function in stress distribution in the language.

A description of stress placement presupposes, in part, a knowledge of grammatical structure. In Chapter III it was assumed that the grammar provides the necessary syntactic and semantic information whereby positions of accents of varying degrees within a sentence can be specified. Accented positions were shown to represent the boundaries of phonological phrases, i.e., the domains within which lower-level, rhythmically-motivated stresses are distributed. The sample analysis to be presented in the rest of this study is intended to propose a way in which it can be shown that syllables in strong metric position generally obtain their metric prominence-signalling capacity by being assigned stress of some degree essentially through ordinary stress-placement processes. This amounts to the supposition that quantitative prosody, like prosody in any other verse type, is in a broad sense, an aspect of linguistic competence, whatever its relationship to musical principles might be.

We have seen in Chapter II that the adoption by Hungarian prosodists of the classical quantitative model, rather than the Western European formula based on stress, has resulted in a verse type in which stress and metric peaks are not systematically co-ordinated. It follows that the system of normal stress placement in the language by itself is insufficient as a crieterion by which the appropriateness of the occurrence of a given syllable in ictus may be determined. This system implies a correspondence of sense and accentuation, and hence it must be modified or supplemented in order for stress to be shown as a fundamental rhythmic component in a verse tradition where metrically forced rhythmic peaks are not necessarily semantically justified.

Accordingly, the analysis presented here is based on two closely related concepts. First, the notion of *stress placement* is understood to be a part of the concept of grammar: a speaker places stresses within a grammatically-semantically defined domain by reference to certain stress rules such that the resulting stress configuration will be consistent with the semantic interpretation of the sequence of elements within the domain, as well as with all meta-theoretical constraints on stress placement in the language. In Chapter III a somewhat detailed account of part of this process was presented with respect to Hungarian. Stress contours obtained through this process may be regarded as being stylistically neutral or unmarked. Thus the line

10. a bú:ču: tördelt hángja:t rébegè:m

represents a perfect correspondence of ictus and positions of stress (of some degree); that is, the abstract metric formula is fully actualized by the stress-determined rhythmic configuration of the filling language material: line 10 is an unmarked line.

The second concept to be utilized here is that of *stressability*, which involves an extension of certain principles that govern the occurrence of stress under normal conditions, to an explanation of verse-governed rhythmic behavior. By relying on the concept of stressability, we are able to explain in part at least the psychological reality of the metric-rhythmic prominence of certain linguistically unstressed (long or short) syllables. The stressability principle implies that the occurrence in ictus of certain syllables that are not assigned stress by ordinary stress placement rules (or for 'logical' reasons) may still be considered legitimate and justifiable on a stress basis, provided that there exist syllables in formally analogous positions within syntactically definable domains in ordinary discourse which *are* normally stressed. Thus we are supposing that one can encode and decode certain semantically deviant rhythmic patterns by a direct analogy to 'well-formed', semantically motivated patterns, perhaps much in the same manner as some types of syntactically ungrammatical strings are apparently processed and interpreted mentally.[1] We have already discussed briefly some examples illustrating this principle (p. 57); we have noted that the concept of stressability is based on two general tendencies in Hungarian. First, it involves the tendency of syntactically and semantically closely related words to merge or fuse into phonological phrases and thus to function from the point of view of stress placement as if they were single words. Secondly, this principle makes explicit the stress potential of the underlying lexical sources of phonological phrases. In either way, inherent principles of the language are utilized, but they are extended to account for the behavior of language under highly specialized conditions such as in verse, and specifically for the occurrence of normally unstressed syllables in strong metric positions in a semantically anomalous verse tradition. We shall say that such syllables receive *metrically motivated* stress which can be said to be stylistically marked.

An analysis of Hungarian iambic verse on the basis of these two system-related principles yields some rather substantial evidence in support of the hypothesis postulated earlier in this paper: iambic verse sounds natural and is readily acceptable to a native audience because, perhaps unaware of doing so, poets succeeded to a great extent in adjusting the borrowed quantitative principle to the available prosodic resources in the language: they could ignore strong accents but they could not help co-ordinating in an overwhelming majority of metric lines metric rhythm peaks with syllables which they intuitively and unknowingly judged to have natural prominence potentials—by virtue of being not only long (and often even only short) but stressed or stressable. As a matter of fact, contrary to claims reviewed in Chapter II, even the dislocation of strong accents in instances other than those explained by the principle of stressability shows a remarkable pattern: the appearance of strong accents in weak position is most common immediately after a major break, especially the beginning of a line. Since there is a strong tendency in Hungarian to begin a sentence with a strong accent, and major breaks generally signal the beginning of a new sentence, in this particular metric context poets failed to reconcile language and meter: in such cases the metrically forced iambic rhythm is clearly artificial and counter-intuitive,[2] although one can learn and come to expect it, as indeed many generations of speakers of Hungarian have done just this. In the present analysis, this type of discrepancy between accent and metric sP's will be taken to represent the phenomenon of *artificial prominence shift* (i.e., an artificial matching of linguistic prominence [by accent] and metric prominence [by ictus] in favor of the latter).

Of course, such a shift is hardly ever made in actual recitation, except if one wishes to disregard the language of verse and 'rhythmicize' instead, like children often do. Performing a line of verse in such a way that the pre-learned 'beat' overrides the countering rhythmic effect of the language of the line is equivalent to producing the same beat by tapping, clapping, whistling, or any other similar non-linguistic means. This sort of rhythmicization is of neither metric nor linguistic interest; it is simply the physical realization of an abstract rhythmic *structure,* similar to ones that the poet attempts to fill by meaningful syllable sequences.

To be sure, ideally there should be a one to one correspondence between linguistically prominent syllables and metrically prominent positions. We judge the rhythmic function of metric language *with respect to the metric pattern.* We take for granted cases of complete correspondence between linguistic rhythm and metric rhythm, and are possibly aware only of cases of non-correspondence; for in every such instance we must make a decision whether to break some linguistic rules in order to conform to the underlying metric pattern, or to break the pre-established abstract rhythm in order to avoid violating linguistic rules. The incompatibility of the two superimposed rhythmic patterns is the potential source of metric *tension.* In actual performance (recitation) we generally resolve the tension in one way or another;[3] in metric analysis we must account for its exact causes.

In this analysis we shall assume that every syllable in sP is stressed: some of these syllables normally carry (linguistically assigned) stress, while others are stressed *only* because the meter requires them to be. In other words, we proceed as if iambic lines had only one surface representation, that corresponding to the underlying iambic schemes. By keeping variables such as the inversion and substitution of metric feet constant, we are enabled, without resort to any manipulation of the metric frame, to investigate the consequences of an extreme hypothetical situation, and to inquire whether occurrences of stress that appear to be metrically motivated exclusively are linguistically justifiable at all. In actual performance meter and language interact in a complex and subtle way, so that the conditions which determine the perceptual prominence of certain syllables are extremely difficult to specify with accuracy. Furthermore, by approaching the selected corpus of data on a formal linguistic (rather than phonetic) basis, we are able not only to distinguish stylistically unmarked and marked stress contours, and to account (by reference to the concept of stressability) for the occurrence of normally unstressed syllables in ictus, but we are also equipped to explain in a principled way the intuitively felt difference within the set of marked forms between the linguistically plausible and the artificially superimposed.

The analysis of the text given in the Appendix is based on the three concepts just noted. The system of stress placement is primary: it implies a grammar and hence a theoretical framework. The notions of stressability and artificial prominence shift presuppose normal stress distribution and serve mainly as additional analytical criteria.

Preliminary analysis

A chief underlying motivation for this study is the evident failure of the musical-quantitative concept to be supported by the very facts that are customarily cited in its support. Perhaps the most remarkable aspect of this failure is the conspicuous rarity of metric lines which display a regular alternation of short and long syllables. It must be emphasized once again that the internal structure of the abstract metrical formula is one kind of *fact*, and the precise manner in which the formula is linguistically realized in a given instance, is another; the two are not to be confused. Similarly, that poets thought they were writing pure quantitative verse is not the same sort of fact as what they *did* write; and what they wrote can hardly be called pure quantitative verse if such verse is understood to imply compliance with the requirement of regular time-unit alternation. In Chapter II, some statistical figures were given showing the excessive ratio of substitutions in the corpus of lines cited by Horváth. The percentages in the text analyzed here are even higher: irregular long syllables occur in 40 per cent of the first four weak positions, and irregular short syllables appear in 15 per cent of the first four strong positions (where the ultimate and penultimate syllables of a line are not counted). Even more noteworthy is the fact that no more than 5 to 6 per cent of the lines in this corpus are completely regular by strict quantitative standards, and the rest include at least one (but generally more than one) substituted foot. It could be argued then that, strictly speaking, some 95 per cent of the lines do not fully support the quantitative principle; in general, the value of a line as evidence in favor of this principle decreases in proportion to the number of substituted syllables which it contains, since even quantitativists admit that such syllables can achieve their rhythmic function *only* by virtue of being supplemented by stress.

To be sure, such an argument would be taken by quantitative theorists to have no bearing on the validity of the concept of time-measurement as the basis of prosody: substitution on any scale is supposed to be immaterial to verse rhythm, since the ideal rhythmic pattern is said to prevail in any case, even if every syllable in a line is irregular. Yet perhaps we can assume that of all the rhythmically 'irrelevant' syllable structures those bearing a one to one correspondence to the ideal formula are somehow basic; such metrically 'perfect' lines set and maintain, or re-establish from time to time, the expected regular rhythmic flow, and represent a norm with respect to which variations by the substitution, addition, elision, etc. of syllables are recognized. This assumption is, at any rate, not inconsistent with the quantitative concept.

Now, it will be recalled that, according to Horváth, in such regular iambic lines in Hungarian the sole rhythmic component is relative syllable length: stress is irrelevant, and its co-occurrence with metrically prominent long syllables is as best accidental. Thus in the lines (see Appendix)

    17. a nágyvilà:g az é:letĩškolà

   475. a gyö:zedèlmi fé:nyeš ünnepè:jen

where underlined syllables are in ictus, ´ is accent, and ` is secondary word stress, there is a perfect correspondence between (a) syllable structure and abstract formula, (b) stressed syllables and strong positions, and (c) unstressed syllables and weak positions. Yet in the quantitativist interpretation only (a) is considered rhythmically pertinent: the fact that the syllable structures involved are included within meaningful grammatical sequences and are thus subject to stress placement processes is deemed rhythmically inconsequential or ignored altogether. If any systemic relationship is to be supposed between the rhythmic potentials of metric sentences and 'inherent rhythmic tendencies' of the language, however, it cannot be shown on any other basis except by reference to the entire linguistic system: time-defined syllable length artificially separated from the very feature that ties it to the grammar, i.e., stress, is evidently not a sufficient point of systemic reference. It is for this reason that the quantitative concept is inherently non-linguistic and that quantitativist references to rhythmic potentials of the *language* amount to vague and unsupported assertions. It is for the same reason that this concept is forced to rely heavily on manufactured artifacts such as syllable length 'defined by position' (as opposed to being defined 'by nature')[4] such as *nagyv* in line 17 where "the vowel remains short but the time devoted to the pronunciation of the following two consonants assures the length of the syllable."[5] A similar artifact is 'length by a following pause' as the final *a* in line 17. There would be no need for such manipulations if it were recognized that successful iambic verse in Hungarian is a far cry from the prosody of Classical Greek: the ancient quantitative *formula* survived but its musically conceived prosodic principle cannot be expected to be in complete harmony with rules of a music-independent natural language. *nagyv, a,* and all other metrically prominent syllables in 17 and 475 are naturally perceived by listeners as being prominent simply because their prominence is assured by linguistic *stress,* as well as the meter.

It goes without saying that a line does not need to have a quantitatively regular syllable structure in order for its stress contour to correspond to the metric rhythm. For example, we have seen that in

   10. a b<u>ú:č</u>u: t<u>ö</u>rdelt h<u>angja</u>:t r<u>é</u>bege<u>:</u>m

stress and ictus coincide throughout the line, although all but the first and last feet are quantitatively irregular. In many other instances, the stress contour and the meter only partially correspond within a line, as in

   185. bé<u>se</u>:dei<u>k</u>re ri<u>f</u>ka:n f<u>é</u>lel<u>è</u>k

where the stress on *bé* in the first metric position (henceforth P1), which is a weak position (wP), is dislocated with respect to the following strong position (sP). In the rest of the line, stress and meter match.

Since the principal aim of this study is to argue for the fundamental significance of stress in this prosodic system, metric lines or parts of lines which display such a correlation between stress occurrence and metric rhythm, regardless of their quantitatively defined syllable structure, are the most obvious evidence in support of the argument. Note that in the examples cited above (except 185), all sP's are filled by a syllable that is either accented, and therefore phrase-initial, or stressed, and therefore included within a phonological phrase to which the rule (25') in Chapter III applies. Furthermore, stress is assigned by (25') to syllables in all sP's (except the last) uniquely, since the phrase boundaries would prevent the placement of stress on a syllable adjacent to an accent. The syllables in many ultimate sP's may not be uniquely stressed but are capable of being assigned stress. Such syllable sequences having metrically unmarked stress contours will be taken for granted in this analysis and left unanalyzed.

There will be one exception to this, incidentally, which ought to be noted in passing. The corpus includes several words whose stressed syllables coincide with sP's (and whose stress contour is thus metrically unmarked) but which make up syllable-sequence *units* (see below) with some other, usually syntactically related, word(s) that, their stressed syllables being in wP, can be accounted for only in terms of the former. For instance the word *anynyisor* in line 23, considered by itself, is metrically unmarked, since S1 is in sP, S2 is in wP, and S3 is in sP, and hence stress and ictus coincide. On this ground, this word should be omitted from the list of marked forms. But it is closely tied to the immediately following word *kina:lt* (adverb-verb) the S1 of which is in wP and in which therefore stress and ictus do not coincide. Since the two words function metrically as a single unit, they will be listed as such. The same consideration applies to words such as *bese:deikre* in 185 where, strictly speaking, only the first two syllables should be listed as being metrically marked, since the second sP is filled by the stressed syllable *ikr*.

More crucial for purposes of the present argument is a detailed examination of those lines in the corpus in which the function of stress as a rhythmic component is not immediately obvious. Thus within the strict quantitativist framework of reference, stress is claimed to be inherently irrelevant to the rhythmic actualization of *quantitatively regular* syllable sequences, although it is admitted that stress becomes functional as a rhythmic element in proportion to the degree to which the syllable structure of a metric line deviates from the ideal metric pattern. Let us consider, then, some additional syllable sequences which, like the lines 17 and 475, fully conform to the underlying quantitative pattern. In the following, underlined syllables are those in sP, / and + mark major and minor boundary,[6] ´ and ` mark primary and secondary accent, and parenthesized words indicate relevant contexts. Capital letters refer to categories to be discussed below.

    74. mágvait vète:d   (A)

    16. nágy vìla:got   (B)

    97. mit féje:re (tett)

  287. ném e:gete: (meg)   (C)

  106. léhajtom   (D)

    64. béle:peregnek   (E1)

    58. póha:rt èmelve   (E2-3)

  148. séke:rre (ùltek)   (E4)

  299. míe:rt (a jóg)   (E5)

    33. /tíed /háza:m   (F)

176. +gyákorta (mègrohan) (G)

487. (midö:n) élö:sör (ültünk) (H)

In all these cases, regular short-long syllable alternation alone is supposed to realize the metric rhythm, since every sP is occupied by a long syllable and every wP by a short syllable, while linguistically placed stress may or may not coincide with metrically prominent positions. More precisely, it is *accents* that may or may not support the metric rhythm; for, in the light of the distinction made in the previous chapter, once the positions of accent are known, further stress distinctions are automatically made on the basis of the principles expressed in the word stress placement rule (25'). Due to the nature of stress distribution in the language, secondary stress occurs (or may occur) on alternate syllables before and after an accent; thus where the accent coincides with a strong metric position, the distribution of adjacent stresses is perfectly consistent with the regularly alternating iambic pattern. The only legitimate basis on which the role of stress in this verse type may be questioned is the fact that accented syllables often occur in wP, and consequently the adjacent syllables in sP are unstressed. This, in fact, is in the center of the quantitativist argument against stress.

What is not taken into account in this argument, however, is the nature of the *conditions* under which discrepancies between accented syllables and the meter seem to occur. The list of examples just given illustrates the type of general conditions involved: note that, with the exception of the residual group (H), an accented syllable not in sP meets at least one of the following specifications: it

(a) bears a secondary accent

(b) is or is preceded by a monosyllable

(c) is preceded by a boundary

Let us briefly examine these conditions. (a) applies, for example, to (A) and (E2-3). The constituent structure is (object) *noun-verb* (or verbal) in 74 and 58. By the rule (2) in Chapter III, the first member of each grammatical phrase is assigned primary accent and the second member may or may not carry secondary accent. In principle, it is the task of the grammar to specify the conditions under which secondary accent occurs; since a grammar is assumed here, it will be sufficient to note that such accent may or may not be present in a particular instance. The point to emphasize, however, is that any secondary accent is necessarily *linguistically* weaker than primary accent, whatever its phonetic correlate may be in a given case.[7] The difference in degree between the two accents is thus formally defined primarily on grounds of syntactic structure, and hence all weak accents assigned to certain syllables in metric sentences can be treated alike in a principled manner.

Specifically, it appears that weak accents so defined are easily suppressed in favor of compliance with metric rhythm—easily because their omission does not bring about the same counter-intuitive effect as does the shifting of primary accent from a first to a second syllable, and indeed such an omission is often very natural. Thus it cannot be said that the appearance of a weak accent in wP under such conditions adversely affects the established rhythm since such an accent is generally capable of being subdued without a gross violation of the semantic givens involved.[8] We shall say that the resulting stress contour is metrically marked. Specifically, the omission of the weak accent in *ve* in 74, for example, will amount to the elimination of a phrase boundary. Consequently, the entire sequence will function as a single phrase, to be labelled a *metric phrase*, which will be subject to stress placement by (25′) like a phonological phrase. Schematically, in 74, (marking strong and weak accent by 1 and 2 respectively)

$$\text{\#magvait \# vete:d\#} \longrightarrow \text{\#magvait vete:d\#}$$
$$\quad 1 \qquad\quad 2 \qquad\qquad\quad 1 \quad 3 \quad 4$$

Similarly, in 58,

$$\text{\#poha:rt \# emelve\#} \longrightarrow \text{\#poha:rt emelve\#}$$
$$\quad 1 \qquad\quad 2 \qquad\qquad\quad 1 \qquad 3$$

By this principle, the long syllables *it+v, e:d,* and *elv* in sP in the respective examples are assigned secondary phrase stress. (The problem of accented *po* in the first wP of the line will be taken up below.) Note that we obtain metrically marked stress contours by means of an ordinary stress placement rule of the language: it is the *domain* of stress assignment that we have modified, but did so by applying a *single* principle formulated on a syntactically reasoned, purely linguistic basis.

Condition (b) applies to (B) and (C). In each case, a word made up of any number of syllables is preceded by a monosyllable with which it may or may not be in a constituency relation. Accent occurs on either the monosyllable or the S1 of the following word. The accented syllable may be in sP (B) or wP (C).

Cases such as 16 where the monosyllable and the following word constitute a grammatical phrase (*adjective-noun*) and (the S1 of) the first member is in sP are similar to those discussed in (a): secondary accent on the second S1, if it occurs at all, is omitted and the whole unit becomes a metric phrase subject to (25′). The chief motivation for this particular interpretation of this unit type is, of course, the correspondence of ictus and primary accent. Thus in 16, we obtain

$$\#\underline{nagy\,\#vila\!:\!got}\# \longrightarrow \# \underline{nagy\ vila\!:\!got}\#,$$
$$\quad\;\, 1 \quad\; 2\quad\; 3 \qquad\qquad 1 \qquad 3$$

although the stress pattern on the right side of the arrow is common in normal discourse, and hence in many cases it can be treated as being metrically unmarked. In (C), however, where there is a similar modifier-modified constituent structure involved, the modifying (and hence strongly accented) monosyllabic member is in wP. Yet the unaccented first syllable of the modified element is rendered metrically prominent without force. Since only quantitatively regular lines are being considered here, the most immediately available explanation is that prominence is assured by syllable length. Yet short syllables are capable of accomplishing the same.

The explanation seems to lie in the underlying stress-potential of the syllable involved: *any first syllable,* including monosyllables, is potentially stressable in Hungarian by virtue of its underlying lexical stress. Thus the syllable *e:g* in (C) above (line 287) legitimately fills an sP by bearing stress which is *metrically motivated but linguistically plausible:* I will refrain from asserting that such stress is linguistically 'permissable' since such an assertion would imply that the grammar contains some optional rule whereby such stress is assigned. Current notions of 'grammar' and 'linguistic competence' are limited to those aspects of a speaker's linguistic knowledge that bear on the correlation of sound and meaning. Stress for which the sole motivation is metrical is, by definition, sematically unjustified and therefore, to this extent, beyond the scope of grammatical description. It is an open question, however, whether the ability of a native speaker to utilize such resources of his language is not indeed an important aspect of his linguistic competence.

In (C), then, two stressed syllables are juxtaposed: *ném* carries linguistic accent and the following syllable is stressed by virtue of its lexical stress. The common convention in the European metric tradition that of two adjacent stressed syllables either one may be metrically prominent, can be usefully applied to the present interpretation. Note that the relative degrees of stresses involved are irrelevant; since the S1 of the second word is in sP, the linguistic

prominence of the accented monosyllable with respect to the next syllable is
neutralized. The syllable in sP can be regarded as the left-hand boundary of a
metric phrase, and, optionally, *nem* as a pre-phrasal syllable: for example, in
287,

$$\#\text{nem e:gete: meg} \longrightarrow \#\text{nem e:gete: meg}$$
$$\qquad 1 \qquad 3 \qquad\qquad\quad 1 \quad 1 \quad 3$$

$$(\longrightarrow \text{nem } \#\text{e:gete: meg}).$$
$$\qquad\qquad\quad 1 \quad 3$$

Importantly, this process does not change the distribution of secondary stresses.

The same principle applies in reverse to unit types such as that illustrated
by 97 under (B). Here the monosyllable is unstressed and the following syllable
is accented. But a monosyllable is always capable of being metrically prominent
by virtue of its underlying lexical stress. (This is the *sole* reason why short
monosyllables are accepted in ictus in Hungarian.) In this case, the monosyllable
in sP may be said to mark the onset of a metric phrase, and consequently the
following accent is subdued; thus in 97,

$$\#\underline{\text{mit}} \# \text{feje:re (tett)} \# \dashrightarrow \#\underline{\text{mit}\#\text{feje:re}} \text{ (tett)} \# \longrightarrow$$
$$\qquad 1 \qquad 2 \qquad\qquad\quad 1 \quad 1 \qquad 2$$

$$\#\underline{\text{mit feje:re}} \text{ (tett)} \#$$
$$\quad 1 \quad 3 \qquad 2$$

In the same manner, the occurrence of all (short or long) monosyllabic function
words (articles, connectives, relative pronouns, etc.) in sP can be accounted for
by a single principle. Thus one could argue that the difficulty encountered in the
quantitative interpretation, namely, that such occurrences have to be explained
by means of stress in one instance and of syllable length in another, is avoided in
this analysis altogether.

To be sure, this explanation may not appear entirely satisfactory. For
instance, the last example we cited represents a rather artificial rhythmic pattern
from the point of view of ordinary discourse, mainly because the two words
involved here, unlike those in 16 above, are not in a close constituency relation
and do not readily merge into a single phonological phrase. As a matter of fact,
it is likely that as this principle is consistently applied to all corresponding
syllable structures, a similarly artificial pattern will result even in such instances
where there is a close syntactic tie between the monosyllable and the following

word. Thus it may be objected, for example, that, by this principle, in a noun phrase made up of *definite article + noun*, we would be compelled to assign stress to the former, which, however, is normally never stressed. To illustrate, consider line 75:

$$\underline{\text{a gyümölcöt}} \longrightarrow \underline{\text{a gyümölcöt}} \longrightarrow \underline{\text{a gyümölcöt}}$$
$$\;\;1\quad 3 \qquad\qquad 1\;\;1\quad 3 \qquad\qquad 1\quad 3$$

Although there is clear evidence that there are circumstances under which the definite article *is* assigned stress in ordinary discourse in Hungarian,[9] and although probably *any* monosyllable may carry stress of some degree under some conditions, the last phase of the shift sequence in such cases may well be considered objectionable in the light of *normal* stress occurrence in the language.

The concept of stress shift is being proposed in this study on the assumption, however, that the conditions imposed on language by the metric frame are *not* normal, and as a result, certain rules of the language *are* violated. Rules are not broken at random, however; in every instance (save the concept of artificial prominence shift) where metrically marked rhythmic contours are postulated in this study, the basic principle that is being utilized is a linguistic given, a deep-rooted characteristic of the language. We are only assuming that the principle is extended by analogy, and thus we are dealing with controlled deviance of a kind.

Controlled deviance is a trademark of literary uses of language; $\underline{\text{a}}$
                                                                                                            1
$\underline{\text{gyümölcöt}}$ would be a deviant form in normal usage, but it is appropriate in
     3
metrically charged verse (cf. $\underline{\text{a nemjo:ja:t}}$, $\underline{\text{a he:tsa:za:t}}$ etc., mild swear
                                                                $1\quad 3 \qquad 1\quad 3$
expressions in emotionally charged ordinary usage). It will not affect this principle, let us note, that often certain sequences of syllables which do not precisely fit into the metric pattern due to the dislocation of an accented syllable with respect to a sP, are perceived as *gestalts*, i.e., in accordance with what Hungarian prosodists refer to as the 'syllable-gathering principle'. Thus in 97, the three syllables between the two stressed syllables *mit* and *tett,* both in sP, may be processed perceptually as a single unit, such that both the linguistically prominent syllable *fej* and the metrically prominent syllable *e:r* become neutralized and subdued. In either case, the metric equivalence of the line is maintained.

A case related to (C) is that illustrated by 106 (group D). Although single words, units of this type may pattern like those in (C). The constituent structure involved is *prefix-stem.* The only prefixes in Hungarian are verbal prefixes and the superlative prefix *leg-;* the former are all derivational and all but a few exist as independent lexical items (originally all verbal prefixes were adverbs). Furthermore, all the stems are free. Thus the prominence of an accented prefix can be metrically neutralized by providing metrically motivated stress on the S1 of the stem, i.e., in 106,

$$ \text{le} + \underline{\text{hajtom}} \longrightarrow \text{le} + \underline{\text{hajtom}} $$
$$ \quad 1 \qquad 3 \qquad\qquad 1 \quad\ 1 $$

We have already seen (Chapter III, footnote 34) that sometimes in such words word stress shifts from the prefix to the stem.

Forms in (E), (F), and (G) are subject to the condition (C): in all three groups, each unit contains an accented syllable in wP immediately following a boundary. Furthermore, the accented syllable is the S1 of a polysyllabic word. In order for the iambic rhythm to be realized, the accent must shift from S1 to S2. This, however, results in a gross violation of the rule (4) in Chapter III. There is no doubt that discrepancy between accent and meter, the (partial) incompatibility of the ascending type of iambic rhythm with the essentially descending rhythmic tendency in Hungarian, is the most obvious in this metric context. That, in spite of this conflict, iambic meter became the most popular verse form in modern Hungarian poetry may well be due to the fact that such dislocations are generally limited to the context following a boundary—exactly the same place where inverted feet are most common in metric traditions. The boundary most often involved is the beginning of a line: the substitution of a trochee for an iamb in the first foot, very frequent in English and German for example, means that the rhythmic onset of the iambic line is actually *descending,* and only the second (usually obligatorily) regular iambic foot establishes the dominant pattern. Less frequently, the same phenomenon occurs after caesurae within lines (but rarely near the end of a line). Occasionally, even Hungarian poets (including Petőfi whose poetry is the source of the corpus treated here) consciously used such 'choriambic' patterns (i.e., long-short-short-long syllable sequence, and hence a rhythmically descending foot followed by an ascending foot) at the beginning of a line. The point is that a descending rhythmic onset following a boundary, especially in the first hemistich, is legitimate in iambic verse, no matter what the organizing principle may be. Insofar as such an inversion after breaks is permissible, the concept of 'artificial prominence shift' in the opposite direction could be dropped altogether. We are retaining the concept, however, since it allows us to pinpoint the only case of incompatibility between the iambic pattern and the Hungarian language.

Note, then, that in *all* the following instances the only stressed syllable dislocated with respect to a sP is immediately preceded by a boundary. Thus, in (E), at the beginning of a line,

64. ((béle:peregnek ⟶ ((belé:peregnek
         3   3

58. ((póha:rt emelve ⟶ ((pohá:rt emelve
          3   3

148. ((séke:rre ültek ⟶ ((seké:rre ültek

299. ((míe:rt a jóg ⟶ ((mié:rt a jóg

Similarly, in (F), after a caesura,

33. /tíed /háza:m ⟶ /tiéd /hazá:m

and in (G), after a minor boundary (i.e., between two major constituents),

176. +gyákorta mègrohan ⟶ +gyakórta mègrohan

It should be observed that the application of this principle logically follows the distribution of metrically motivated stresses in accordance with the principles (a) and (b). This order is logical because the shifting of stress *within* a phrase, as in 58, presupposes stress on S1; if condition (c) were to apply before condition (a), for example, then there would, of course, be no stress on S1 after the application of (c).

In the foregoing, we have considered some quantitatively regular syllable sequences, and have attempted to show that even in such metrically perfect units time-defined syllable alternation is by no means the sole rhythmic factor, since such alternation corresponds to a very large extent to configurations of potential stress occurrence. The examples that we have discussed are representative of the major categories into which the complete corpus has been analyzed. The various unit types included in the respective categories show that, in general, syllable sequences comprising like or comparable *syntactic* structures fulfill (or may fulfill) identical rhythmic functions *regardless of the length values* of the syllables that they contain, although, for obvious reasons, the correlation between long syllables and sP's is fairly extensive.

We may schematically represent the internal structure of the metric units in each of the analytic categories illustrated above. Thus *magvait vete:d* (line 74) exemplified the group (A), subgroup (2) (see Groups in Appendix). In (A1), the constituent structure is *noun - verb*; the first constituent is invariably three syllables long, and the second constituent is at least two but no more than three syllables long (i.e., the third syllable may or may not be present: we shall include such syllables in parentheses); ordinarily, that is, by the rule (2) in Chapter III, primary accent (´) is on the S1 of the first constituent, and secondary accent (ˋ) is on the S1 of the second constituent; finally, the S1 and S3 of the first constituent are in sP (marked by underlining). Using the abbreviations N, V, and VP for noun, verb, and verb phrase, respectively, we can express all the above by the following general formula:

$$(A1): \quad \left\{ \; [\underline{\acute{S}} \, S \, \underline{S}]_N \quad [\; \grave{S} \, \underline{S} \, (S)]_V \right\} \; VP$$

Each of the illustrative examples that we have discussed in this chapter may be represented in a similar manner. To assure optimal generality, we shall disregard category symbols, and indicate "any number of syllables optionally" by the symbol (S_i) (the subscript "i" for 'indeterminate').

GROUP	STRUCTURE
(A)	$\left\{ [\underline{\acute{S}} \, S \, \underline{S}] \; [\grave{S} \, (\underline{S}) \, (S_i)] \right\}$
(B)	$\left\{ [\underline{\acute{S}}] \; [\grave{S} \, (\underline{S_i})] \right\}$
(C)	$\left\{ [\acute{S}] \, [\underline{\grave{S}} \, (S_i)] \right\}$
(D)	$\left\{ [\acute{S}\text{-}] \, [\underline{\grave{S}} \, (S_i)] \right\}$
(E)	$((\left\{ \acute{S} \, \underline{S} \, (S_i) \right\}$
(F)	$/ \left\{ \acute{S} \, (\underline{S_i}) \right\}$
(G)	$\left\{ [\acute{S} \, \underline{S} \, (S)] \; [\underline{\grave{S}} \, (S_i)] \right\}$

Procedure

The analysis of the selected groups (Text) consists of a categorization of all syntactically or morphologically defined syllable-sequence units which have metrically marked stress contours. The categorized lists (Groups) as well as the Text (and its translation into English) appear in the Appendix. In the preceding preliminary analysis examples illustrating the structure (unit-) types included within the major groups were given and three general principles were formulated and justified:

(a) omission of secondary accent

(b) utilization of underlying lexical source

(c) artificial prominence shift

It was suggested that by means of these principles all cases (except for a small residue) of discrepancy between linguistic rhythm and verse rhythm can be accounted for. These principles apply to the major groups A - H in the following manner: [10]

A1-7	(a)
B1-12	(a), (b)
C1-8	(b)
D1-2	(b)
E1	(c)
E2-3	(a), (c)
E4	(c)
E5	(c)
E6	(a), (c)
F, G	(c)

The group H, although exhibiting a certain pattern, is best considered residual.

Each line in the text has been analyzed by the following criteria, applied in this order:

Do accents and sP's coincide?

1. if yes, rule (25′) applies and assigns stress to syllables in sP (unmarked stress contours). Such lines are left blank.

2. if no, determine the group membership of the deviant syllable-sequence unit. Supply appropriate group reference under the line (marked stress contours).

We have already seen that, within 2, the order in which the rules and principles apply is significant. For example, in (E2) and (E3), the principle (a) applies first, eliminating the secondary accent from the S1 of the second member and turning the entire unit into a metric phrase. Next the S4 of the phrase, being long, is assigned stress by (25a). Now the S1 and S4 of the phrase are stressed, and then by (c) stress is shifted from S1 to S2: now stress and sP's coincide. In the Text, ordering, where relevant, is suggested by the vertical sequencing of symbols.

Source of data

The corpus consists of 589 lines of iambic verse (18 complete poems), taken from the works of the Hungarian poet Sándor Petőfi (1823-1849). The selections were made at random, with the exception that an attempt was made to represent each major period of the poet's work. By coincidence, the data include several line structures (trimeters, tetrameters, pentameters, etc.) and stanza forms,[11] as well as poems of widely different content and intensity. On the whole, the selected corpus can be said to be representative of Petőfi's iambic verse.

However, since this study is concerned with Hungarian iambic verse in general rather than with works of a single poet, the question arises whether the conclusions reached through an analysis of such a restricted body of data can be claimed to have a significant measure of generality. In this connection, the following remarks are in order:

1. Limitations of space obviate a choice between at least two alternate methods of selecting data: one may collect individual lines (out of context) from a variety of poets or take a coherent body of lines from a single source. The first alternative is used by Horváth (see Chapter II). The principal objection to this method is that it does not include any safeguards against subjectivity and arbitrariness (Horváth's honesty and objectivity are not being questioned here; the method itself is unreliable).

2. Some statistical indication was given in Chapter II that the metric lines listed by Horváth in his significant study are generally consistent with the corpus given here. Complete consistency cannot be expected because Horváth cites forms from Gedeon Ráday (mid-1700's) and modern twentieth-century poets under the same heading; yet it is well known that in many respects there is little resemblance between samples of iambic verse produced at respective ends of this 200 year span. During this period, iambic prosody has undergone significant changes, gradually developing from an artificial game that served mainly to satisfy the fancy of fashionable social circles into an expressive form of unprecedented popularity.[12]

3. Petőfi's iambic verse is generally acknowledged to represent the zenith of this development: it marks a turning point, a transition from the conservatively quantitative practices of the eighteenth and early nineteenth century to the freer, less rigid prosody of modern iambic verse. Gáldi notes that "Petöfi retains and in fact respects the established iambic tradition but shapes it to his own image by adding variety to it."[13] It seems to be generally agreed that Petőfi set the stage for the subsequent development and popularity of the iambic form.[14]

In view of the foregoing, the corpus selected for the present purpose is considered sufficiently representative to serve as a basis for the formulation of a general hypothesis regarding the nature of iambic prosody in the Hungarian tradition as a whole. The validity of this hypothesis is, of course, subject to further proof or disproof in the light of evidence produced by subsequent studies.

Summary

The purpose of this study was to inquire whether there was any *a priori* reason for excluding a consideration of stress from the study of Hungarian quantitative prosody in general, and iambic verse in particular. The chief motivation for questioning some basic tenets of the traditional strict quantitative theory was the belief that the rhythmic behavior of language in verse and in normal discourse is subject to the same general underlying principles of the language. The chief rhythmic component of ordinary speech is stress which, where non-distinctive, tends to coincide with syllable length. Thus the hypothesis was postulated that time-measured syllable alternation in Hungarian iambic verse (as a typical test case) is significantly supplemented by stress occurrence that can be characterized on the grounds of grammar-related stress-placement processes in the language. Syllable sequences involving discrepancies between accent and ictus were considered legitimate domains of (low-level) stress assignment by the same general rule, on account of the shiftability of the left-hand domain boundary from an accented syllable to one carrying metrically motivated stress by virtue of its underlying lexical stress. Metrically (i.e., stylistically) unmarked and marked stress contours were distinguished, and arguments in favor of the linguistic reality and acceptability of the latter were given. In view of the evidence presented, it might be reasonable to conclude that stress is a relevant rhythmic factor in Hungarian iambic (and presumably all other types of quantitative) verse, and its exact role deserves further exploration and research.

NOTES

1. See Chomsky 1965, p. 149.

2. Horváth flatly denies this: the iambic rhythm in Hungarian can be 'descending' many a time as regards stress "without its time measurement ceasing to be genuinely iambic" (1955, p. 77).

3. Fónagy (1959, pp. 152-59) has performed some interesting experiments on various aspects of performance with bearing on the problem of metric tension. Instrumental evidence based on verse recitals by noted Hungarian actors seems to indicate that metric prominence is often signalled by raised pitch rather than stress, while positions of accent (in weak metric positions) continue to be marked by stress. Thus stress and pitch, which ordinarily co-occur, become separated, pitch fulfilling the metric function and stress the semantic function. For an interpretation of metric verse from the viewpoint of melody and music, see László 1961.

László argues, incidentally, that "rhythm and melody form an inseparable unit" (p. 15), and the "object of research can only be verse that is correctly reproduced and made audible and animated" (p. 13). Performance as the basis for metric analysis has been a controversial issue in metric study; the inherent dangers in proceeding from data obtained through performance are magnified when historical factors are involved. For example, certain long vowels in Hungarian have shortened since Petőfi's time (Sebeok 1943; G. Varga 1968).

4. This terminology is in common use in traditional descriptions, borrowed from classical metrics. Syllable length 'by nature', i.e., phonemic long vowels, is a clear case, but the concept of length 'by position' is dubious. The syllable pattern VCC is a legitimate linguistic entity in the language provided the two consonants are included within a single phonological phrase (in which case the presence of an intervening word boundary is irrelevant), as already pointed out in Chapter III. But a syllable defined across a sentence boundary, for example, as in tied vagyok#tied (line 33) appears to have no psychological

reality. In fact, the quantitative postulation of this artifact weakens the theory, as much as it supports it. For long syllables so defined by position are very common in weak positions (e.g., legtöbbsör čendes/ne:ma, line 182, where *weak* positions are underlined), resulting in 'spondees' and hence forcing the theory to admit stress as the sole rhythmic determinant. Stress, of course, occurs in the respective syllables in ictus *in any case,* and the absence of stress on the adjacent syllables uniquely qualifies those syllables to fill weak positions. For a recent re-examination of syllable length in Hungarian, see Kecskés 1966, p. 126.

5. Horváth 1955, p. 71.

6. The terms are used in a loose sense here. The beginning of a line following an end-stopped line, for example, would be considered a major break (i.e., boundary), since it probably signals the beginning of a new sentence or clause. Caesurae within lines also represent major boundaries. Minor boundaries occur between lower-level constituents where for reasons such as inverted word order, insertion, etc., a slight pause is called for.

7. Secondary accent may in fact be *phonetically* stronger in some instances than a neighboring primary accent, even when the former is not emphatic or contrastive accent, or not due to the 'logical' importance of the word involved. Phonetic realizations are an aspect of linguistic performance and have little or no bearing on the abstract relations which define the system of stress placement. See Chomsky and Halle 1968, Part II. We are assuming here that the relationship between primary and secondary accent within a syntactically defined constituent is specified by a *general* rule in the language, to which there may be certain well definable exceptions.

8. In ordinary discourse in Hungarian, the shift of stress to the following (otherwise unstressed) syllable *within* a stretch of speech appears to be less deviant than a similar stress shift after a major boundary. Since in Hungarian stronger stresses tend to be located near boundaries, it may be that the weaker the stress the more easily it shifts since the less significant it is semantically and hence the less difference its presence or exact position makes.

9. For example, in a phrase such as *a te bára:tod* 'your friend' where the definite article *a* is actually a pre-phrasal syllable S-3 (see Chapter III), and therefore may be assigned secondary stress; thus #*a te # bara:tod* #. It is clear
$$\underset{3}{} \quad \underset{1}{} \quad \underset{3}{}$$
that the stressedness or non-stressedness of an article or any other function word is by no means a purely semantic problem.

10 The labelling of the groups (A-H) and the numbering of the subgroups are arbitrary; the arrangement of the subgroups has no significance. Because of the limited amount of data examined here, the constituent structures associated with particular subgroups are only rough approximations; several subgroups include 'loose' forms (marked †) with analogous structure and metric behavior, for which separate subclasses were deemed unnecessary.

11. Naturally, only very few of the 155 stanza forms that Petőfi used (Horváth 1955, p. 74) occur in the corpus treated in this book.

12. For details, see especially Négyesi 1892 and Horváth 1951.

13. 1955, p. 581.

14. For a comprehensive bibliography on Petőfi's verse, see Szathmary 1961, pp. 669-72. Also cf. Tezla 1964.

APPENDIX

SYMBOLS

Letters(spelling)	Transcription	Pronunciation
a	a	[ɔ]
á	a:	[a:]
b	b	[b]
c	c	[tˢ]
cs	č	[tˢ̌]
d	d	[d]
e	e	[ɛ] ~ [æ]
é	e:	[e:]
f	f	[f]
g	g	[g]
gy	gy	[dʸ]
h	h	[h]
i	i	[i]
í	i:	[i:]
j	j	[y]

k	k	[k]
l	l	[l]
ly	j	[y]
m	m	[m]
n	n	[n]
ny	ny	[nʸ]
o	o	[o]
ó	o:	[o:]
ö	ö	[œ]
ő	ö:	[oe:]
p	p	[p]
r	r	[r]
s	š	[š]
sz	s	[s]
t	t	[t]
ty	ty	[tʸ]
u	u	[u]
ú	u:	[u:]
ü	ü	[ʉ]*
ű	ü:	[ʉ:]*

v	v	[v]
z	z	[z]
zs	ž	[ž]

*high front rounded vowel
Note: *au, eu* are diphthongs (*u* is non-syllabic); doubled consonants (*pp, nyny,* etc.) mark phonemically long consonants.

Additional symbols:

)) right-hand boundary

(filled) context, not part of unit

/ major syntactic boundary (caesura)

+ minor syntactic boundary (secondary pause)

- morpheme boundary within a word

† item is exception to category but follows pattern

GROUPS

$$(A) : \left\{ [\acute{S} \, S \, \underline{S}] \quad [\grave{S} \, (\underline{S}) \, (S_i)] \right\}$$

A1 adverb or adjective - verb

23.	anynyisor kina:lt	'has offered so often'
26.	oj gyakran dagadt	'has so often swollen'
101.	hastalan kerešlek	'I look for you in vain'
227.	egyara:nt vehet	'can take equally'
229.	egyara:nt foglal (hejet)	'are seated equally'
319.	ne:p köze: vete:tek	'threw among the people'
352.	ba:rmike:nt kiva:nom	'how much I may wish'
362.	hastalan ešengek	'I implore in vain'
405.	jo:kedvvel vesen	'takes in good cheer'
411.	rettentö: lesen	'shall be terrible'

(A2) noun - verb

74.	magvait vete:d	'sowed its seeds'
223.	millio:k ca:folnak	'millions disprove'
290.	eledelt kiva:nt	'needed only food'
301.	-izzada:š čorog	'sweat drips'
377.	sikla:va: kövül	'turns into a rock'
589.	hi:veid vala:nk	'we are your faithful'

(A3) possessor noun - possessed noun

27.	senvede:š emle:kzete:t	'memory of suffering'
28.	sent öröm könyü:je	'tear of a sacred joy'
271.	e:letünk nese:t	'a sign of our life'
285.	do:ža györgy hire:t	'George Dozsa's fame'
318.	alkotma:ny ro:ža:ja	'rose of the Constitution'
370.	mult idö:m emle:ke	'memory of my past'
397.	-ha:boru:k törte:nete	'history of wars'

(A4) noun - postposition or pronoun

106.	ši:rhalmod felett	'above your grave'
† 118.	te:gedet nekem	'you, to me'
119.	valakai maga:t	'somebody. . . himself'
122.	(borbe:j)mü:hejek elö:tt	'in front of the (barber)shops'
142.	ša:torok alatt	'under the tents'
209.	ka:naa:n fele:	'toward Canaan'
447.	fellegek közü:l	'from among the clouds'
533.	aka:cfa:k alatt	'under the acasias'
† 585.	a:ldozunk neked	'we're paying sacrifice to you'

(A5) adjective - polysyllabic noun

15.	va:ltozo: serenče	'changing fortune'
41.	(össe)roškado: kebel	'collapsing heart'
73.	izzado: fejembe	'into my sweating head'
103.	hallgatag fele:ben	'in its silent midst'
110.	epedö: sava:t	'its imploring word'
154.	megsakadt felhö:kben	'in its broken clouds'
222.	semtelen hazugša:g	'impertinent lie'
263.	legkišebb serep	'smallest role'
270.	ma:šodik somse:dig	'to the second neighbor'
273.	fekete meze:t	'its black garment'
371.	(leg)borzasto:bb alak	'(most) terrible shape'
455.	a:tkozott neved	'your cursed name'

(A6) adjective - monosyllabic noun

82.	megve:nült e:v (/so:lta:l)	'aged year, (you spoke)'
86.	haldoklo: e:v (ši:rod)	'dying year, (your grave)'
† 109.	ajakam so:l))	'my lips speak'
177.	e:hezö: vad (/me:rgeš-)	'starving beast, (raging)'
413.	jövendö: kor (jelenen:šei)	'(visions) of a future age'

(A7) mixed residue

4.	išmerd meg fiad	'recognize your son'
96.	elte:pted honomnak	'you tore up my nation's'
105.	küsöbe:t a:tle:pem	'I step across its threshold'

164.	va:lassunk magunknak	'let's choose for ourselves'
166.	vissa fog vezetni	'it will lead back'
244.	kiš vila:g maga	'itself a little world'
315.	adjatok jogot	'give rights'
344.	ešniök tala:n	'that they fall perhaps'
354.	ijenkor sivembe	'at such times into my heart'
376.	ige:it fülembe	'its words into my ears'
404.	se:p la:nyto:l vira:got	'flower from a fair maiden'
453.	ta:volbo:l elö:re	'from far away in advance'
459.	ho:dolo:d ele:g les	'followers you'll have plenty'
463.	föld ele:dbe	'the earth in front of you'
488.	gyorš idö: fölöttünk	'fast time above us'
509.	adna:m e:n oda	'I would give it up'

$$(B) : \left\{ [\acute{S}] \; |\grave{S} \; (\underline{S}_i)] \right\}$$

(B1) adjective - noun

	8. V(e:) betü:je	'letter "V" '
	11. jo: anya:nak	'of the good mother'
	16. nagy vila:got	'wide world'
	28. sent öröm	'sacred joy'
	29. la:gy öle:n	'on its soft bosom'
	32. se:p haza:m	'my fair land'
	48. nagy vila:gon	'in the wide world'
	52. jo: idö:ben	'in good weather'
	59. u:j fe:nyt	'new light'
	62. telt üvegnek	'of the full bottle'
	77. rešt munka:latomnak	'my lazy labor'
	81. (meg)gyu:lt vila:ga	'its ignited world'
	99. sebb reme:nyeimnek	'of my better hopes'
	120. ru:t idö:t	'ugly weather'
	129. nagy le:ptekkel	'with long steps'
†	152. ne:gy ökör	'four oxen'
	155. bu:š hölgy	'sad lady'
	167. mu:lt idö:knek	'of past times'

201. sent fa:t	'sacred wood'
† 243. öt vila:gre:s	'five continents'
243. nagy terü:lete:n	'great expanse'
244. kiš vila:g	'little world'
268. nagy hamar	'in a great hurry'
315. sent neve:ben	'in its sacred name'
317. u:j ve:doslopot	'new column of support'
370. mult idö:m	'my past'
404. se:p ja:nyto:l	'from a fair maiden'
407. sent sabadša:g	'sacred freedom'
416. kis menynydörge:š	'little thunder'
434. gaz hazugša:g	'evil lie'
464. sent napo:leon	'sacred Napoleon'
466. se:p seli:d semed	'your tender pretty eyes'
488. gyorš idö:	'fast time'
495. ke:k eget	'blue sky'
560. zöld širunkra	'upon our green grave'

(B2) **adjective - adjective**

19. oj göröngyöš, oj keme:ny	'so jerky, so hard'
26. oj gyakran	'so often'
74. oj šok	'so much'
146. ij rege:nyeš	'such romantic'
283. mij sörnyü:	'how terrible'
548. oj rege:nyeš	'so romantic'

(B3) **adverb - verb**

153. fenn vala	'was up'
159. ott vale:k	'I was there'
172. u:gy le:zengek	'I loaf just like'
233. itt van	'is here'
277. u:gy ragyog	'shines so'
288. u:gy vigya:zzatok	'be so careful'
313. u:gy futott	'ran so'
430. u:gy van	'it is so'
474. ott lesek-e	'will I be there'
477. ott lenn	'down there'
482. ott kia:ltšatok	'shout there'

492. i:gy rezgette:k   'shook thus'
511. u:gy bušultam   'I grieved so'
† 529. se:p legyen   'that it be beautiful'

(B4) pronoun - verb

 21. e:n tudom   'I know'
208. ö:k vezešše:k   'that they lead'
310. ezt ke:rdeznem   'my asking this'
355. te hoza:d vala   'you brought'
384. mit hasna:l   'what's the use'
430. ö:k bese:lik   'they say'
471. te sa:modra   'for you'
480. az lesek   'I will be that'
575. mi vagyunk   'we are'

(B5) possessor noun - possessed noun

 78. hi:r čillagja   'fame's star'
172. ö:s vira:ga   'autumn's flower'
224. nap heve:ben   'in the sun's heat'
316. hon neve:ben   'on the nation's behalf'
372. bor heve:tö:l   'from wine's heat'
485. si:v pora:ra   'to the heart's dust'

(B6) negative particle - verb

 46. nem kia:ltom   'I do not announce it'
 94. nem figyelve   'ignoring'
118. nem mutat   'will not show'
† 139. ninč ugyan   'though there isn't'
146. nem törte:nnek   'do not happen'
183. nem tudom   'I don't know'
198. nem tuds   'you cannot'
† 234. ninč megnyugva:š 'there is no stopping'
257. nem akarom   'I do not want it'
279. nem hagyna:m   'I would not leave'
297. nem kerü:lheti   'cannot avoid'
317. nem nyer   'does not win'
361. nem feled   'does not forget'

385. nem jut   'does not occur'
387. nem hallhatni   'cannot be heard'
425. nem gyu:jt   'does not ignite'
433. nem bi:r, nem akar   'it cannot, it does not want to'
504. nem panaslok   'I do not complain'
578. nem lobogna   'would not fly'

(B7) noun - postposition

 85. si:v felett   'over the heart'
319. ne:p köze: 'among the people'
390. ešt között   'between . . . and evening'
481. föld alatt   'under the earth'
487. to: fölött   'above the lake'
487. fa:k alatt   'under the trees'
497. vi:z felett   'above the water'

(B8) mixed residue

 12. ma:r re:gen   'already long ago'
 54. ešt közelget   'the night nears'
 78. ra:m šuga:rt vetett   'cast its ray upon me'
 97. mit feje:re   'which upon its head'
168. šorš egyma:što:l   'fate (us) from each other'
196. az maga:ra   'that one upon himself'
197. mošt keze:be   'now into its hand'
273. gya:s š gyala:zat   'mourning and shame'
291. me:g a:llat vala   'it was still animal'
312. ma:r emle:ksobort   'yet a monument'
389. fa:k merengve   'trees, musing'
468. azt silaj kezed   'that your violent hand'
510. le:gy mellettem   'be next to me'
588. mi uto:šo: 'we the last'

(B9) conjunctives, articles, pronouns

 61. egy čeppig bora:t   'its wine to the last drop'
126. e:š haši:t   'and is splitting'
143. e:š bemegy   'and enters'

148. e:š azon mene:nek	'and went thereupon'
149. de ökörseke:ren	'but on an ox cart'
184. e:š megso:li:t	'and addresses me'
272. kik rea:nk ke:si:tik	'who are preparing for us'
306. kik vallja:tok	'(you) who claim'
307. e:š mienk	'and ours is'
308. de vite:zek	'but they are brave'
360. egy sellemnek	'of a spirit'
372. egy pokoli	'of a devilish'
437. mint bora	'like its wine'
504. mert amenynyit	'for as much as'
530. e:n elö:sör	'I the first time'
532. ö:t elö:sör	'her the first time'
540. hol kigyu:ladt	'where it caught fire'
558. ha letesnek	'when they set (me) down'
570. ha:t ke:tše:gbe	'in despair though'

(B10) 'hogy' - predicate

47. /hogy te vagy	'that you are'
82. /hogy ne e:gjen	'that it not burn'
181. /hogy bele:	'that into it'
232. /hogy mega:lljunk	'that we stop'
257. /hogy šajna:ljatok	'that you feel sorry for me'
275. /hogy magyar vagyok	'that I am Magyar'
293. /hogy legyen joga	'that it have rights'
327. /hogy mulaššanak	'that they live it up'
586. /hogy a:lda:šod	'that your blessing'

(B11) 'is' - verb, 'sem' - verb

132. (mit) iš tegyen	'what else could he do'
189. (azt) šem tudom	'I don't even know'
262. (mi) iš ja:tsottunk	'we too played'
276. (nem) iš hajnallik	'isn't even dawning'
303. (ke:z) iš kell	'hands too are needed'
346. (akkor) iš sent les	'it will be sacred even then'
554. (ez) iš	'this too'

(B12) **definite article - noun**

22.	a tapastala:š	'experience'
24.	a hala:lt	'death'
75.	a gyümölčöt	'fruit'
80.	a šorš	'fate'
83.	a vad la:ng	'wild flame'
87.	a reme:ny	'hope'
91.	a buču:t neked	'farewell to you'
116.	a menynyben tala:lkozol velem	'you meet me in heaven'
117.	a menynyorsa:g	'heaven'
121.	a se:l	'wind'
121.	a ta:nye:r	'disk'
123.	a boldogša:g	'happiness'
137.	a va:ndorsine:s	'travelling actor'
141.	a ciga:ny	'gypsy'
143.	a se:l	'wind'
144.	a ciga:ny	'gypsy'
151.	a seke:rrel	'cart'
153.	a hold	'moon'
157.	a somse:d mezö:kön	'neighboring meadows'
158.	a füvektö:l	'grasses'
179.	a šorš	'fate'
193.	a reme:nyek	'hopes'
200.	a vila:gnak	'world'
205.	a la:ngoslopot	'column of flame'
213.	a ne:p	'people'
238.	a hala:l	'death'
241.	a föld	'earth'
248.	a föld	'earth'
252.	a mošoj	'smile'
254.	az öröm	'joy'
265.	a villa:mot	'lightning'
265.	a gyerek	'child'
266.	a magyar	'Magyar'
277.	a nap	'sun'
278.	a vila:gon	'world'
289.	e la:ng	'flame'
292.	az a:llatbo:l	'animal'
295.	a legru:tabb	'ugliest'

300. a haza:t	'nation'
301. a ne:p-izzada:š	'people's sweat'
303. a földet	'earth'
304. az arany ere	'vein of gold'
309. az ellenše:g	'enemy'
314. az emberiše:g	'mankind'
318. a tie:tek	'yours'
321. a töviš fele:t	'half of the thorns'
334. a čata:ban	'battle'
341. a ruha:k	'dresses'
369. a telt	'filled'
370. a mult	'past'
383. a kinom	'my pain'
386. a bu:š	'sad'
390. az idö:	'time'
402. a sabadša:g	'liberty'
403. a harcte:rre	'battlefield'
409. a čata:knak	'battles'
435. a nyelvetek	'your tongue'
425. a haragoš	'angry'
431. a magyar	'Magyar'
436. a magyar	'Magyar'
446. a hüvejbö:l	'scabbard'
452. a ra:ko:ciak	'Rakoczi's'
460. a magašbo:l	'high above'
465. a kerek vila:got	'round world'
467. a seretet	'love'
470. a diadal-i:v	'arch of triumph'
478. e nagy	'great'
483. a respublika:ra	'republic'
547. a delet	'noon'
567. a magyart	'Magyar'
577. a šöte:tše:g	'darkness'
578. a mi fe:nyünk	'our light'
581. a vila:g	'world'

(C) :   [Ś] [Ṣ̀ (Sᵢ)]

(C1) adjective - noun

32. hü: gyermekedre	'onto your faithful child'
60. sent e:letedre	'onto your sacred life'
83. vad la:ng	'wild flame'
87. la:gy bölčeje:ben	'in its soft cradle'
196. nagy munka:t	'a great task'
219. nagy gonoson	'in a very evil way'
239. la:gy čo:kkal	'with a soft kiss'
261. nagy tetteidet	'your great deeds'
267. holt dičö:še:g	'dead glory'
313. hö:š la:bnak	'to the heroic foot'
323. se:p ri:m-š-me:rte:kbe	'into pretty rhyme and meter'
393. kis feleše:gem	'my little wife'
† 502. ke:t e:ve	'two years ago'
527. zöld fürteiteken	'on your green limbs'
557. se:p arany	'pretty gold'

(C2) adjective - adjective

405. oj jo:kedvvel	'in such good cheer'
490. ij ö:s	'such autumn'
517. oj dra:ga	'so dear'
529. oj se:p	'so beautiful'

(C3) adverb - verb

264. u:gy rettege:	'so afraid was'
† 276. itt mina:lunk	'here at us'
280. hö:n seretem	'I deeply love'
334. ott a:llok	'there I stand'
494. igy tükröze:	'so it reflected'
496. igy ringato:zott	'so was it being rocked'
530.* itt la:ttam	'here I saw'
534.** itt ült	'here she sat'

*Also 532
**Also 535

(C4) pronoun - verb

35.	kit seretne:k	'whom would I love'
120.	az hozta	'that's what brought'
219.	azt hirdetik	'that's what they preach'
308.	mit tenne:tek vajon	'what would you do'
457.	azt bečülik	'that's whom they respect'
470.	te le:s	'you shall be'
512.	azt gondolhatna:k	'that's what they might think'
542.	ez volt	'this was'
573.	ez le:gyen	'let this be'

(C6) negative - verb or noun

	21.	nem tudja	'does not know'
	36.	nem seretne:lek	'would not like you'
	45.	nem mondom	'I am not telling'
	71.	nem foglak	'I will not'
†	77.	nem rešt	'not lazy'
	82.	ne e:gjen	'that it not burn'
	98.	nem i:rlak	'I am not recording you'
	115.	nem adja:k	'they are not giving'
	144.	nem so:l	'is not saying'
	145.	nem pešten	'not in Budapest'
	164.	ne va:lassunk	'shall we not choose'
	181.	ne le:pjen	'that he not step'
	183.	nem e:lek	'I am not alive'
	194.	ne fogjon	'let him not set to'
	200.	ninč ra:d	'there is not of you'
	237.	nem fog	'will not'
†	244.	ninč anynyi	'there is not that many'
	263.	nem volt	'was not'
†	276.	nem is	'not even'
	284.	nem ke:r	'it will not ask'
	285.	nem hallotta:tok	'have you not heard'
	287.	nem e:gete:	'did not burn'
†	326.	nem henye	'not lazy'
	330.	nem čeng	'is not ringing'
	330.	nem dörg	'is not thundering'
	341.	nem a (ruha:k)	'not (dresses)'

342. nem ke:rdem   'I am not asking'
350. ne ba:ntšon   'let it not hurt you'
352. nem lehetek   'I cannot be'
† 355. nem te   'not you'
364. nem enged   'will not let me'
378. ne so:li:tš   'do not speak to me'
424. nem lobbans   'will you not explode'
436. nem pežg, nem habzik   'it is not sparkling, not foaming'
466. nem te:ri:t   'will not convert'
478. nem e:rem   'I will not see'
500. nem čo:kolhattam   'I could not kiss'
543. nem e:keši:te   'did not adorn'
† 548. nem oj   'not so'
552. ne fe:lj   'do not fear'
565. nem vi:vta   'did not win'
587. nem e:rdemetlen   'not undeserved'

(C7) **interjectives**

4. oh išmerd   'oh recognize'
86. oh haldoklo: 'oh dying one'
170. be somoru: 'how sad'
345. hadd eššenek   'let them fall'
407. oh sent   'oh sacred'
426. oh nemzetem   'oh my nation'

(C8) **mixed residue**

55. nö: bu:m   'my gloom is growing'
193. me:rt čalnak   'why do they deceive'
229. mind egyara:nt   'all equally'
246. van rajta   'it has on it'
266. mi moštan   'what is now'
270. hogy hallgatunk   'how silent we are'
282. mošt adjatok   'give now'
302. mit e:r   'what is it worth'
311. majd elfeledtem   'I almost forgot'
322. föl tudna:m   'I could . . . up'
339. mind ba:tran   'all bravely'
390. de:l š ešt   'noon and evening'

406. ha:ny dra:ga	'how many dear'
454.* mošt ho:dolok	'I am paying tribute now'
458. mošt üdvözöllek	'I am welcoming you now'

*Also 458

$$(D) : \left\{ [\acute{S}\text{-}] \quad [\text{-}\underline{S}(S_i)] \right\}$$

(D1) **verbal prefix - verb stem**

12. se:t-hordoza:k	'spread out'
40. el-döntöm	'I demolish'
61. ki-hajtom	'I empty'
81. meg-gyu:lt	'ignited'
83. ki-holt	'became extinguished'
84. el-hamvadt	'burned out'
100. ki-e:gett	'burned out'
102. meg-la:tjuk	'we see it'
105. a:t-le:pem	'I step across'
106. le-hajtom	'I bow'
107. föl-e:bredends-e	'will you wake up'
119. meg-ölte	'he murdered it'
143. be-megy	'it enters'
174. meg-sa:radt	'dried-out'
181. meg-tiltja	'it forbids'
184. meg-so:li:t	'it addresses'
220. meg-a:llhatunk	'we may stop'
232. meg-a:lljunk	'that we stop'
264. ki-ra:ntott	'grabbed out'
268. föl-föltünik	'it keeps emerging'
268. le-bu:vik	'it pulls back into hiding'
286. el-e:gete:tek	'you burned it'
300. meg-serze:k	'they acquired it'
303. ki-ha:nyja	'shovels it out'
304. föl-tü:nik	'it suddenly appears'
317. el-dö:l	'it falls'
324. meg-la:togatni	'to visit'
343. tu:l-e:lnek	'they survive'

368. meg-jelenik	'it appears'
368. meg-a:ll	'it stops'
368. meg-jelenik	'it shows up'
375. fel-feltör	'it keeps ascending'
401. meg-vi:ni	'to fight'
445. el-rablott	'it stole'
445. el-temetett	'it buried'
465. el-foglalod	'you occupy it'
484. meg-hallom	'I hear it'
505. el-vitt	'it took away'
540. ki-gyu:ladt	'it caught fire'
546. le-tü:nt	'it disappeared'
547. meg-e:rtem	'I have reached'
554. el-jö:	'it will come'
558. le-tesnek	'they place me down'
563. el-zu:gtak	'they swept by'
564. le-čendesü:lt	'it has quieted down'

(D2) superlative prefix - adjective stem

47. leg-kedvešebbem	'my dearest'
182. leg-többsör	'mostly'
242. leg-sebb	'most beautiful'
254. leg-jobban	'best'
295. leg-ru:tabb	'ugliest'
366. leg-e:dešb	'sweetest'
371. leg-borzasto:bb	'most terrible'
457. leg-jobban	'most, best'

(E): (([Ś S̲ (Sᵢ)]

(E1) four-syllabic or longer (single word)

6. a:rnye:kain (/uto:sor)	'(last) in its shadows'
18. veri:te:kembö:l (ott)	'of my sweat (there)'
47. legkedvešebbem (hogy te)	'the dearest to me (that you)'
64. bele:peregnek))	'drop into(it)'
70. le:lekzete:vel (e:let-)	'with its breath (life-)'

77.	jutalmau:l (nem rešt)	'as a reward (for not lazy)'
90.	somse:dša:ga:ban (ijen)	'near (such)'
107.	föle:bredends-e (ekkor)	'will you wake up (then)'
124.	bara:tša:goš (/meleg)	'friendly, (warm)'
125.	/napsa:mošne:))	'female farm hand'
185.	bese:deikre (ritka:n)	'to their talk (rarely)'
162.	bese:lgete:nek (š e:nek-)	'were chatting (and singing)'
207.	la:ngoslopoknak (rendele:)	'(ordered to be) flame columns'
225.	ke:tše:gbeešve (tengenek)	'desperately (carry on)'
240.	vira:gköte:llel (/šejem-)	'by flowered rope, (silk-)'
268.	föl-föltünik (š lebu:vik)	'keeps appearing (and vanishing)'
275.	se:gyenlenem (kell, hogy)	'I (must) be ashamed (that)'
281.	gyala:zata:ban (iš /nemzet-)	'(even) in its shame, (my nation)'
294.	/emberjogot (a ne:pnek)	'human rights (for the people)'
300.	apa:itok (megserze:k)	'your fathers (acquired)'
308.	haza:tokkal (mit tenne:tek)	'with your land (what-)'
319.	tövi:šeit (a ne:p)	'its thorns (the people)'
329.	la:togato:ba (ja:rjanak)	'(that they pay) visits'
335.	katona:id (közt /sa:zadom)	'(among) your soldiers, (my company)'
343.	tu:le:lnek-e (majd engemet)	'will they survive (me)'
364.	ke:rlelhetetlen (/šiket)	'implacable, (deaf)'
368.	megjelenik (/kezem)	'it appears, (my hand)'
397.	sabadša:gha:boru:k	'freedom fights'
410.	halottaide:rt (bossut)	'for your dead, (revenge)'
412.	ve:rpanora:ma (leng)	'blood-panorama (appears)'
421.	riadjatok (meg /haršona:k)	'blow, (trumpets)'
443.	vila:graso:lo: (hi:redet)	'your world-wide (fame)'
448.	vaku:ljanak (meg /š meg-)	'let them get blind (and they do)'
450.	respublika (/sabadša:g)	'republic, (freedom's)'
453.	kösöntelek (a ta:volbo:l)	'I greet you (far away)'
465.	elfoglalod (majd a)	'you will conquer (the)'
480.	republika:nuš (vagyok)	'(I'm) republican'
497.	a:bra:ndošan (a viz)	'dreamily (the water)'
565.	sabadša:ga:t (nem vi:vta)	'(it didn't win) its freedom'
572.	ellenkezö:leg (/oh hon)	'on the contrary, (oh my land)'

(E2) two-syllabic adjective - noun

1.	arany kala:ssal	'with golden wheat'
8.	va:ndor daru:id	'your migrating cranes'
23.	šöte:t poha:rbo:l	'from a dark glass'
31.	vida:m napod (-)	'your gay sun'
42.	ve:gšő: ima:ja	'its last prayer'
73.	magaš tervektö:l	'from high plans'
93.	ba:gyadt seme:t (-)	'its tired eyes'
97.	ifju: reme:nye	'its young hope'
104.	halva:ny šuga:rt (a hold)	'a faint ray (the moon)'
114.	keblem tüze:tö:l	'from my heart's heat'
127.	daro:c po:ja:ban	'in a fancy blanket'
134.	kopott guba:ja:t	'his worn-out belongings'
139.	meleg ruha:ja	'warm clothes'
157.	kalma:r sellö: (ja:rt)	'light breeze (moved)'
178.	e:les körme:t (-)	'its sharp nails'
191.	e:deš reme:ny (tart)	'sweet hope (keeps)'
199.	šaja:t fa:jdalmad	'your own pain'
206.	u:jabb idö:kben	'in recent times'
242.	magyar vagyok (/)	'I am Magyar'
255.	magaš kedvemben	'in my high mood'
272.	šaja:t testve:rink	'our own brothers'
286.	izzo: vaštro:non	'on a glowing iron throne'
296.	išten teremtme:nye:n	'on god's creature'
297.	išten keze:t (el nem)	'god's hand (it can not)'
337.	harcos lege:ny (-)	'fighting fellow'
338.	rongyoš lege:nyek	'ragged fellows'
347.	meghalt esme:im	'my dead ideas'
374.	ezen sellemnek	'to this spirit'
379.	e:deš hangod (šem)	'(nor) your sweet voice'
394.	egyik kezemben	'in my one hand'
396.	ma:šik kezemben	'in my other hand'
398.	minden betü:je	'its every letter'
414.	saja:t ve:rök (tava:ba)	'their own blood's (lake)'
441.	minden čepptö:l (az)	'from every drop (the)'
462.	/dičö: respublika	'glorious republic'
492.	seli:d fuvalmak	'tame breezes'
524.	vida:m dalošmada:rto:l	'from gay birds of song'
526.	örök tavas (lakozze:k)	'(let) eternal spring (reside)'
531.	kedveš galambomat	'my dear love-dove'

569. magyar keze:ben   'in the Magyar's hand'

(E3) two-syllabic adverb or noun - verb

†	2. mejnek fölötte	'above which'
†	7. fejem fölött (/mi:g)	'over my head, (while)'
	33. tied vagyok (/tied)	'yours am I, (yours)'
	49. titkon kiše:rem	'I secretly follow'
	58. poha:rt emelve	'raising a glass'
	92. rea:d függeste:	'it cast upon you'
	95. ekke:p felelte:l	'you answered thus'
	99. hova: leve:l (/te)	'where have you gone, (you)'
	100. kora:n kie:gett	'perished too soon'
	106. fejem lehajtom	'I bow my head'
	126. tuško:t füre:sel	'sawing a log'
†	141. /vacog foga	'his teeth are chattering'
†	160. vale:k somse:dja	'I was a neighbor to'
	188. gyakran bojongok	'I often loaf'
†	212.* a:tok rea: (/ki)	'cursed by (who)'
†	231. ragyog minden (ha:z)	'shines upon every (house)'
	232. akkor mondhatjuk	'then we may say'
	242.** magyar vagyok (/ . . .)	'I am Magyar'
	258. /büske:n tekintek	'I proudly glance'
	289. išme:t pusti:that	'it may again devastate'
†	294. jogot teha:t (/ember-)	'rights, then, (human-)'
	298. mie:rt vagytok (ti)	'why are (you)'
	312. mikor emeltek	'when are you building'
	356. hogyan serezne:l	'how would you cause'
†	363. /hagyjon magamra	'that it leave me alone'
	368. /kezem mega:ll	'my hand stops'
	387. halkan bese:lget	'it is chatting quietly'
†	399. nyargal kerestül	'gallops across'
†	419. legyünk ve:gte:re	'let us finally be'
	506. te:ged hozott (meg)	'it has brought you'
	536. itten röpült (seme:bö:l)	'that's where (from her eyes) flew'
†	546. letü:nt imma:r (e)	'fallen is now (this)'
†	564. se:gyen rea: (/le-)	'shame on it, (down)'
†	582. tekintš rea:nk (/tekintš)	'glance at us, (glance)'

*Also 214.
**Also 250, 258, 266, 274.

(E4) three-syllabic (single word)

3. enyelgve (ü:z/)	'sensuously (plays)'
4. išmers-e (me:g)	'do you (still) know me'
13. azo:ta (hossu)	'since then (a long)'
26. mejektö:l (si:vem)	'from which (my heart)'
32. sentegyha:z (keblem)	'a holy church (is my heart's)'
38. olta:ra (ke:ped)	'(your picture) its altar'
40. eldöntöm (e:rted)	'I shatter (for you)'
44. a:lda:ša (ra:ja)	'its blessing (on it)'
50. mindegyre (hi:ven)	'steadfast (faithfully)'
61. kihajtom (egy)	'I empty (to one)'
66. gyilkolja:k (egyma:št)	'they're killing (one another)'
69. /haldoklo: (/hervadt)	'dying one, (your wilted)'
76. la:thatva:n (/rajta)	'seeing, (over it)'
84. elhamvadt (üske)	'burned-out (cinder)'
93. /šohajto: (nemzetem)	'(my) sighing (nation)'
101. kerešni (foglak)	'(I will) look for you'
119. megölte (valaki)	'(someone) has murdered'
132. ki:nja:ban (ma:št)	'in its pain (what else)'
136. hidegtö:l (fojnak)	'from the cold (running)'
137. barangol (a va:ndor)	'roaming (the traveller)'
143. kopogtat (a se:l)	'knocking (the wind)'
148. seke:rre (ültek)	'on a wagon (they got)'
149. seke:ren (mentek)	'on a wagon (they went)'
153. vila:goš (e:j)	'bright (night)'
154. halva:nyan (ja:rt)	'faintly (moved)'
156. ši:rhalma:t (kereši)	'its grave (seeks)'
171. mio:ta (eltemette:k)	'since (they buried)'
179. kia:ltok (a šorš)	'I shout (fate)'
182. legtöbbsör (čendeš)	'mostly (quiet)'
186. örültem (egykor)	'I was glad (once)'
189. bojongok (/mi:g)	'I roam (until)'
192. reme:lem (/hogy)	'I hope (that)'
202. pusta:ban (bujdošunk)	'in the desert (we hide)'
203. ne:pe:vel (mo:zeš)	'with his people (Moses)'
204. követte (/mejet)	'and followed (that which)'
205. veze:rül (/a la:ng)	'for a guide, (the flame)'
210. elö:re (ha:t)	'forward (then)'

213. keze:bö:l (a ne:p)   'from its hand (the people's)
217. pihenjen (ö:/)   'that (he) rest'
222. hazugša:g (/semtelen)   'lie, (an impertinent)'
227. mindenki (egyara:nt)   'everyone (equally)'
249. kerešne: (/ojan)   'were seeking, (so)'
252. ajkamra (fel-fel)   'on my lips'
260. egekbe (nyu:lo:)   '(reaching) into the skies'
262. euro:pa (si:npada:n)   'on Europe's (stage)'
291. mivelhogy (akkor)   'since (then)'
293. emberhez (illik)   '(it is proper) to man'
321. vegye:tek (vissa)   'take (back)'
336. cata:zok (verseimmel)   'I battle (by my poems)'
345. cata:ban (/a:m)   'in the battle, (well)'
354. nyugtasson (meg)   'let it console you'
358. ege:sen (ma:š)   'quite (different)'
367. e:rinti (ma:r-ma:r)   '(almost) touches'
375. fel-feltör (hozza:m)   'keeps ascending (to me)'
382. körü:lem (ijen)   'around me (such)'
383. miatta (me:giš)   'because of it (still)'
385. esembe (nem jut)   '(it doesn't) occur to me'
392. keblemre (hajtva)   '(laying) on my bosom'
404. e:rette (/mint a)   'for its sake, (like)'
417. villa:mok (futnak)   'lightning (runs)'
427. örökke: (fe:ken)   '(hold back) forever'
433. harcolni (nem)   'to fight (it cannot).
434. hazugša:g (/senynyeš)   'lie, (dirty)'
439. ve:rünket (/ba:rčak)   'our blood, (oh if only)'
450. /sabadša:g (gyermeke)   '(child of) liberty'
451. sabadša:g (anyja)   'freedom's (mother)'
474. seretne:m (tudni)   'I would like (to know)'
477. enye:set (/š ott)   'extinction, (and there)'
479. bara:tim (/emle:kezzetek)   'my friends, (remember)'
483. širomna:l (e:ljent)   '(hurrah) at my grave'
484. meghallom (e:n azt)   'I will hear (that)'
489. azo:ta (ke:t e:v)   'since then (two years)'
491. mošojgo: (ö:si)   'smiling (autumn)'
499. e:lveztem (menyny-)   'I enjoyed (my heaven)'
507. reme:nyim (fe:nyeš)   'my hopes' (bright)'

509. ezerser (adna:m)   '(I'd give) a thousand times'
510. maradjunk (me:g)   'let's stay (yet)'
513. ve:getlen (boldogŝa:gomon)   '(over my) boundless (happiness)'
521. titeket (ültetett)   '(planted) you'
522. harmatnak (ŝ napŝuga:rnak)   'dew's (and sunshine's)'
523. a:lda:ŝa (rajtatok)   'blessing (onto you)'
525. reskeŝŝen (a:gatok)   '(let) your limbs (tremble)'
537. sivembe (serelem)   'into my heart (love)'
541. serelmem (hajnala)   'my love's (dawn)'
547. mege:rtem (a delet)   'I have reached (noon)'
551. serelmem (alkonya)   'my love's (twilight)'
553. ima:dott (assonya)   'beloved (woman)'
561. ŝöte:tke:k (e:jeken)   'at dark blue (nights)'
562. euro:pa (ĉendes)   'Europe (is quiet)'
563. elzu:gtak (forradalmai)   '(its revolutions) are gone'
566. maga:ra (hagyta:k)   '(they left) to itself'
574. emelje (ez fel)   'let (this) raise'
589. egyetlen (hi:veid)   '(your) only (believers)'

(E5) two-syllabic (single word)

  5. /midö:n (e jegenye:k)   'while (under these acasias)'
  9. midö:n (az ö:ŝi)   'while (the ancient)'
 21. /mike:p (nem tudja)   'like (doesn't know)'
 43. a:lda:ŝ (a honra)   'blessing (on the nation)'
 53. /midö:n))   'while'
 98. eze:rt (nem i:rlak)   'that's why (I do not write)'
109. /amit (majd ajakam)   'what (my lips will)'
155. mike:nt (a bu:ŝ)   'like (the sad)'
165. so:le:k (e:n a:bra:ndozva)   'so I speak (dreamily)'
174. egy-egy (megsa:radt)   'a few (dried)'
180. amej (az embernek)   'which (to man)'
181. hanem (megtiltja)   'but (forbids)'
201. aze:rt (a sent)   'therefore (the sacred)'
236. tala:n (az e:let)   'perhaps (life)'
239. seli:d (/la:gy ĉo:kkal)   '(by a) tender (soft kiss)'
241. boĉa:t (le a föld)   'lowers (down in the earth's)'
245. aha:ny (a se:pŝe:g)   'as many (are the beauties)'
263. mienk (nem volt)   'ours (was not)'

271. alig (/hogy küldjük)	'(we) barely (send)'
299. mie:rt (a jog)	'why (the rights)'
304. ami:g (föltü:nik)	'until (it appears)'
307. mienk (a haza)	'ours (is the land)'
314. jogot (a ne:pnek)	'rights (for the people)'
316. amej))	'which'
317. eldö:l (ha nem nyer)	'falls (unless it gains)'
320. ide (a ro:ža)	'here with (the rose's)'
333. hejett (most esme:k)	'instead (now ideas)'
366. /midö:n (a ke:j)	'while (pleasure)'
366. sokšor (/midö:n a)	'often, (while)'
386. bese:l (a fa:kkal)	'speaking (to the trees)'
400. arany (čal /s oštor)	'gold (tempts and whip)'
405. šebet (/hala:lt oj)	'wounds, (death, so)'
408. tie:d (a diadal)	'yours (is victory)'
420. ele:g (volt ma:r a)	'enough (already of)'
423. haza:m (/tova:b is)	'my country, (still)'
437. čendeš (/de tüzeš)	'quiet (but fiery)'
446. jöjjön (ki kardod)	'let (your sword) come (out)'
454. /midö:n (me:g messe)	'while (still far away)'
455. midö:n (me:g re:meš)	'while (still terrible)'
456. midö:n (me:g aki)	'while (still,who)'
464. mike:nt (egy u:j)	'like (a new)'
473. aka:r (a ve:rnek)	'or whether (in blood's)'
482. jertek (ki hozza:m)	'come (out to me)'
488. röpü:l (a gyorš)	'flying (the fast)'
495. vize (a tista)	'its water (the clear)'
508. kie:rt (az örök)	'for whom (eternal)'
518. kedveš (fa:k /üdvözölve)	'dear (trees, blessed)'
520. a:ldom (me:g azt is)	'I am blessing (even that who)'
528. /mike:nt (az)	'like (the)'
529. enye:m (/oj se:p)	'mine, (so beautiful)'
538. tudom (me:g /hogyne)	'I know (still, of course)'
544. te:ged (/te ve:ghetetlen)	'you, (you endless)'
550. mikor (jön majd az)	'when (it will come)'
552. ettö:l (ne fe:lj)	'of this (don't be afraid)'
555. aze:rt (jö: majd /ha)	'that's why (it comes when)'
560. ragyog (le zöld)	'shines (upon green)'
583. išmerd (meg moštan)	'get to know (now)'
584. midö:n (ma:š könynyet)	'while (others even tears)'

(E6) four-syllabic adjective - noun

† 169. va:lastottunk magunknak	'we chose for ourselves'
359. kiše:rteteš halva:nyša:g	'ghostly paleness'
381. irto:ztato: o:ra:ja	'its terrible hour'
† 395. seli:deden hulla:mzo:	'gently waving'

(F) :   /[Ś (S$_i$)]

(F) residual items following major boundary

5. re:g volt /igaz (/)	(E5)	'it was long ago, true,'
33. tied /haza:m))	(E5)	'yours, my country'
56. haza:m /fölötted	(E5,4)	'my country, above you'
67. idö: /sa:rnyadnak	(E5,4)	'time, of your wing'
69. oltšd el (/haldoklo:)	(E5)	'blow out, (dying one)'
91. mondom /tünö: e:v	(E5, 4)	'I say, vanishing year'
144. /sabad))	(E5)	'come in!'
183. e:lek (/nem)	(E5)	'Am I alive? (not)'
250. /terme:setem (+)	(E1)	'my nature'
280. /ima:dom))	(E4)	'I adore'
284. /ragad))	(E5)	'it grabs'
384. /amig (tart)	(E5)	'while (it lasts)'
388. /bese:dire))	(E1)	'to its speech'
390. /nyujto:zom))	(E4)	'I am stretching'
442. šiešš /haza:m /napfe:nyre	(E5, 4)	'hurry, my land, to sunshine'
486. tudod (/midö:n)	(E5)	'you know, (while)'
490. /ijen (se:p)	(E5)	'such (nice)'
552. /sivemnek))	(E4)	'of my heart'
568. /čupa:n (a)	(E5)	'only (the)'
582. /tekintš /sabadša:g	(E5, 4)	'glance, freedom'

(G) : + $\left\{ [\text{Ś} \underline{S} \text{(S)}] [\text{Ś} \text{ (S}_i)] \right\}$

(G1) residual items following minor boundary (phrasals)

3. +tünde:r ja:te:kokat	(E2)	'fairy games'
6. +uto:sor (pihene:k)	(E4)	'I last (rested)'
31. +mosojg išme:t rea:m	(E3)	'smiles at me again'
93. +šohajto: (nemzetem)	(E4)	'my sighing (nation)'

124. +meleg soba:ban	(E2)	'in a warm room'
128. +versenyt visi:t	(E3)	'has a screaming contest'
152. +laššačka:n (ballagott)	(E4)	'slowly (proceeded)'
176. +gyakorta (megrohan)	(E4)	'often (attacks me)'
178. +sivembe (va:gja)	(E4)	'(cuts) into my heart'
180. +menynyet mutat	(E3)	'shows heaven'
217. +a:rnye:k alatt	(E3)	'in the shade'
267. +halva:ny kiše:rtete	(E2)	'its pale ghost'
337. +minden dalom	(E2)	'every one of my songs'
535. +semközt velem	(E3)	'across from me'
568. +minden ke:zen	(E2)	'on every hand'

(G2) residual items following minor boundary (single words)

242. +haza:m))	(E5)	'my country'
250. +komoj))	(E5)	'is serious'
281. +nemzetemet))	(E1)	'my nation'
368. +ijedve))	(E4)	'frightened'
391. +ke:nyelmešen))	(E1)	'comfortably'

(H1) residual items with accent not preceded by boundary

80. sivem šoka:ig (a šorš)	'my heart for long'
88. hahogy sabad (/amit)	'if I may (what)'
88. /amit jövendöl (/hinnem)	'what it prophesies, (believe)'
218. vannak hamiš pro:fe:ta:k	'there are false prophets'
235. addig fojva:št küsködni	'till then constantly to struggle'
246. /amej tekintetet	'which a glance'
259. /ahol semem))	'where my eyes'
274. /š arcom se:gyenben	'my face in shame'
277. holott ma:šhol (ma:r)	'whereas elsewhere'
324. amint illö: (meg-)	'as it is proper (to)'
341. tesi di:se:t (/nem)	'makes its mark, (not)'
365. tala:n örökke:	'perhaps forever'
377. lelkem lelketlen	'my soul a soulless'
380. va:rd el be:ke:ben	'wait it out in peace'
418. ele:g šoka: voltunk	'we have been long enough'
422. elö:l pofoznak (/)	'they're slapping you in front'
449. akik rea:pillantanak	'who glance at it'
469. mejben hala:loš	'in which a deadly'

472. aka:r vira:goš   'whether in a flowery'
486. midö:n elö:sör   'when the first time'
505. šokkal többet hozott   'brought much more'
516. amejeken sivemnek   'on which to my heart'
539. haba:r re:gen vala   'though it was long ago'

(H2) other residue

288. mert az maga tü:z (/)   'because it is itself fire'
290. (a ne:p) hajdan (čak)   '(the people) at one time (only)'
299. (a jog) čupa:n   '(the rights) only'
299. ti-na:latok   'with you'
301. ne:p-izzada:š   'the people's sweat'
384. (a:lom) čupa:n   '(a dream) only'
412. (leng) elö:ttem   '(appears) before me'
418. fa-janko:k   'blockheads'
494. (tükröze:) vissa (a to:nak)   '(reflected) back (of the lake)'

TEXT

The text (lines 1-589) includes eighteen poems by the Hungarian poet Sándor Petőfi (1823-1849), listed below. For page references to source, see Petőfi, 1960, in the *Bibliography*.

The text is given in transcription (see SYMBOLS, p. 91), which reflects the original spelling except where a retention of the latter would lead to confusion. The changes made include the elimination of orthographic double consonants (except "y" which marks palatalized segments) and of certain superfix-like marks (such as that of vowel length, e.g., *á*). Thus every consonant except "y" has a segmental value. Every vowel except the second member of *au, eu* is syllabic and only vowels are syllabic. Since morphophonemic changes are not accounted for, the transcription does not reflect pronunciation.

Further changes include the elimination of capital letters (at the beginning of every line and elsewhere), the reduction of all punctuation marks to "." and ";", and the avoidance of a repetition of identical lines (where repeated lines are omitted, "(. . .)" is used). Words connected by "-" are to be taken as a single word. "**" at the beginning of a line indicates new poem, and "*" marks new stanza.

Lines	Title of poem (and year)	Source page number
1-32	"Hazámban" (In My Country), 1842	8
33-64	"Honfidal" (Patriot's Song), 1844	27
65-98	"Búcsú 1844-től" (Farewell to 1844), 1844	121
99-118	"Hová levél" (Where Have you Gone), 1845	124
119-144	"Téli világ" (Winter World), 1845	137

1.** arany kala:ssal e:keš ro:naša:g,
  (E2   )

2. mejnek fölötte lenge de:liba:b
  (E3   )

3. enyelgve ü:z tünder ja:te:kokat,
  (E4   )   (G1   )

4. išmers-e me:g. oh išmerd meg fiad.
  (E4   )   (C7   )
                    (A7   )

5.* re:g volt, igaz, midö:n e jegenye:k
  (F   ) (E5   )

6. a:rnye:kain uto:sor pihene:k,
  (E1   ) (G1   )

7. fejem fölött mi:g ö:si le:gen a:t
  (E3   )

8. va:ndor daru:id V bctü:je sa:llt.
  (E2   ) (B1   )

9.* midö:n az ö:ši ha:znak küsöbe:n
  (E5   )

10. a bu:ču: tördelt hangja:t rebege:m.

11. š a jo: anya:nak a:ldo: ve:gsava:t
  (B1   )

12. a sellö:k ma:r re:gen se:thordoza:k.
      (B8   ) (D1   )

13.* azo:ta hossu e:všor sületett,
  (E4   )

14. e:š hossu e:všor veste e:letet,

15. š a va:ltozo: serenče sekere:n
     (A5   )

16. a nagy vila:got össeja:rtam e:n.
     (B1   )

17.* a nagyvila:g az e:letiškola.

18. veri:te:kembö:l ott šok elfoja,
     (E1   )

19. mert oj göröngyös, oj keme:ny az u:t,
     (B2   )

20. az ember anynyi šivatagra jut.

21.* ezt e:n tudom, mike:p nem tudja ma:š,
     (B4   ) (E5   ) (C6   )

22. kit üröme:vel a tapastala:š
     (B12   )

23. šöte:t poha:rbo:l anynyisor kina:lt,
     (E2   ) (A1   )

24. hogy ittam volna inka:bb a hala:lt.
     (B12   )

25.* de mošt a bu:t, a hossu ki:nokat,

26. mejektö:l si:vem oj gyakran dagadt,
     (E4   )   (B2   )
                       (A1   )

27. e:š minden senvede:š emle:kzete:t
     (A3   )

28. egy sent öröm könyü:je mošša se:t.
     (B1   )
     (A3   )

29.*   mert ahol enyhe bölčö:m la:gy öle:n
                        (B1   )

30.   az anyatejnek me:ze:t i:zlele:m,

31.   vida:m napod mošojg išme:t rea:m,
       (E2   ) (G1   )

32.   hü: gyermekedre, e:deš se:p haza:m.
       (C1   )   (B1   )

33.** tied vagyok, tied, haza:m.
       (E3   ) (F   )

34.   e si:v, e le:lek.

35.   kit seretne:k, ha te:gedet
       (C4   )

36.   nem seretne:lek.
       (C6   )

37.*   sentegyha:z keblem belšeje,
       (E4   )

38.   olta:ra ke:ped.
       (E4   )

39.   te a:llj, š ha kell, a templomot

40.   eldöntöm e:rted.
       (D1   )
       (E4   )

41.*   š az össeroškado: kebel
        (A5   )

42.   ve:gšö: ima:ja,
       (E2   )

43.   a:lda:š a honra, ištenem
       (E5   )

44.   a:lda:ša ra:ja.
       (E4   )

45.*   de e:n nem mondom šenkinek,
          (C6   )

46.   ki nem kia:ltom,
         (B6   )

47.   legkedvešebbem hogy te vagy
       (D2   ) (B10   )
       (E1   )

48.   a nagy vila:gon.
       (B1   )

49.*   titkon kiše:rem le:pteid,
       (E3   )

50.   š mindegyre hi:ven.
       (E4   )

51.   nem, mint az a:rny az u:tazo:t,

52.   čak jo: idö:ben.
       (B1   )

53.*   de mint az a:rnye:k nö:, midö:n
                          (E5   )

54.   az ešt közelget,
         (B8   )

55.   nö: bu:m, ha šöte:tedni kezd,
       (C8   )

56. haza:m, fölötted.
     (F   )

57.* e:š elmegyek, hol hi:veid

58. poha:rt emelve
     (E3   )

59. a šoršto:l u:j fe:nyt ešdenek
              (B1   )

60. sent e:letedre.
     (C1   )

61.* š kihajtom egy čeppig bora:t
      (D1   ) (B9   )
      (E4   )

62. a telt üvegnek,
     (B1   )

63. ba:r kešerü:, mert könynyeim

64. bele:peregnek.
     (E1   )

65.** egy estendö: a ma:šik ši:rja:t a:šša,

66. gyilkolja:k egyma:št, mint az emberek.
     (E4   )

67. idö:, sa:rnyadnak mc:g egy čattana:ša,
     (F   )

68. š a jelen e:v is ši:rban sendereg.

69. oltsd el, haldoklo:, hervadt ajakadnak
     (F   ) (E4   )

70.   le:lekzete:vel e:letme: čedet,
      (E1   )

71.   nem foglak odai:rni te:gedet,
      (C6   )

72.   hol boldog e:vim följegyezve vannak

73.* magaš tervektö:l izzado: fejembe
      (E2   ) (A5   )

74.   te oj šok esme magvait vete:d,
      (B2)   (A2   )

75.   š e:n a gyümölcöt bö:ven megteremve
      (B12   )

76.   la:thatva:n, rajta büske:n ne:zek se:t.
      (E4   )

77.   jutalmau:l nem rešt munka:latomnak
                    (C6)
      (E1   )   (B1   )

78.   a hi:r čillagja ra:m šuga:rt vetett,
      (B5   ) (B8   )

79.   š e:n me:gšem i:rlak oda te:gedet, (. . .)

80.* sivem šoka:ig a šors balkeze:ben
      (H1   )(B12)

81.   a fa:jdalom meggyu:lt vila:ga volt.
      (D1   )
          (B1   )

82.   te, megve:nü:lt e:v, so:lta:l, hogy ne e:gjen,
      (A6   )   (C6   )
                          (B10   )

83.   e:š so:zatodra a vad la:ng kiholt.
            (C1   ) (D1   )
            (B12)

84.   elhamvadt üske van čak ba:natomnak
      (D1   )
      (E4   )

85.   a rombadö:lt š ma:r fe:l-e:p si:v felett. (. . .)
                              (B7   )

86.* oh haldoklo: e:v. ši:rod mellett engem
      (C7   )
          (A6   )

87.   la:gy bölčeje:ben ringat a reme:ny,
      (C1   )   (B12   )

88.   š hahogy sabad, amit jövendöl, hinnem,
      (H1   )

89.   a menynyorsa:gnak a:llok küsöbe:n.

90.   somse:dša:ga:ban ijen boldog kornak
      (E1   )

91.   mondom, tünö: e:v, a buču:t neked, (. . .)
      (F   ) (B12   )

92.* rea:d függeste: he:vvel ešdekelve
      (E3   )

93.   ba:gyadt seme:t šohajto: nemzetem,
      (E2   ) (E4; G1)

94.   š te so:haja:ra šemmit nem figyelve,
                              (B6   )

95.   ekke:p felelte:l menynydörögve, nem.
      (E3   )

96.   te kosoru:ja:t elte:pted honomnak
              (A7   )

97.   ifju: reme:nye mit feje:re tett.
      (E2   )(B8   )

98.   eze:rt nem i:rlak oda te:gedet, (. . .)
      (E5)(C6   )

99.** hova: leve:l, te sebb reme:nyeimnek
      (E3   )   (B1   )

100. kora:n kie:gett hajnalčillaga.
              (D1   )
      (E3   )

101. kerešni foglak. hastalan kerešlek.
      (E4   )   (A1   )

102. vagy me:g megla:tjuk egyma:št valaha.
              (D1   )

103.* ha majd az e:jnek hallgatag fele:ben
                        (A5   )

104. halva:ny šuga:rt a hold a földre vet,
      (E2   )

105. a temetö:nek küsöbe:t a:tle:pem,
                          (D1   )
                  (A7   )

106. š fejem lehajtom ši:rhalmod felett.
              (D1   )(A4   )
      (E3   )

107.* föle:bredends-e ekkor a:lmaidbo:l,
      (D1   )
      (E1   )

108. e:š elhagyod me:j, hü:vöš nyosoja:d.

109. hogy meghallgašd, amit majd ajakam so:l,
              (E5)   (A6   )

110. a serelemnek epedö: sava:t. (. . .)
              (A5   )

111.* hogy letöröljed lankadt pilla:imro:l

112. az e:rted omlo: könynyek za:pora:t. (. . .)

113.* hogy sellemed majd e:gö: čo:kjaimto:l

114. š keblem tüze:tö:l melegü:ljön a:t.
              (E2   )

115.* vagy holtjokat a ši:rok ki nem adja:k
                          (C6   )

116. š čak a menynyben tala:lkozol velem.
              (B12   )

117. vagy többe: šem az e:j, šem a menynyorsa:g
                          (B12   )

118. meg nem mutat ma:r te:gedet nekem.
              (B6   )   (A4   )

119.** megölte valaki maga:t,
              (D1   ) (A4   )
              (E4   )

120. az hozta ezt a ru:t idö:t.
              (C4   )   (B1   )

121. fuj a se:l, ta:ncol a ta:nye:r
              (B12)   (B12)   )

122.   a borbe:jmü:hejek elö:tt.
        (A4   )

123.   hol a boldogša:g moštana:ban.
        (B12   )

124.   bara:tša:goš meleg soba:ban.
        (E1   ) (G1   )

125.*   a napsa:moš, napsa:mošne:
                              (E1   )

126.   tuško:t füre:sel e:š haši:t.
        (E3   ) (B9   )

127.   daro:c po:ja:ban gyermekök
        (E2   )

128.   a se:lve:ssel veršenyt visi:t.
                    (G1   )

129.*   ja:r nagy le:ptekkel föl-š-ala:
        (B1   )

130.   a katona az ö:rhejen,

131.   e:š sa:mla:lgatja le:pteit,

132.   ki:nja:ban ma:št mit iš tegyen.
        (E4   )   (B11   )

133.*   a hossula:bu dro:tošto:t

134.   kopott guba:ja:t cepeli,
        (E2   )

135.   az orra e:rett paprika,

136.   š hidegtö:l fojnak könynyei.
        (E4   )

137.* barangol a va:ndorsine:s
    (B12   )

138. egy faluto:l a ma:šikig,

139. meleg ruha:ja ninč ugyan,
    (E2   ) (B6   )

140. de mindaza:ltal e:hezik.

141.* ha:t a ciga:ny. . . vacog foga
    (B12   ) (E3   )

142. a rongyoš ša:torok alatt,
        (A4   )

143. kopogtat a se:l e:š bemegy,
    (E4   ) (B12)   (D1   )
                (B9   )

144. ba:r a ciga:ny nem so:l, sabad. (. . .)
        (B12   ) (C6   ) (F   )

145.** nem pešten törte:nt, amit hallotok.
    (C6   )

146. ott ij rege:nyeš dolgok nem törte:nnek.
    (B2   )   (B6   )

147. a ta:ršaša:gnak u:ri tagjai

148. seke:rre ültek e:š azon mene:nek.
    (E4   )   (B9   )

149. seke:ren mentek, de ökörseke:ren.
    (E4   )   (B9   )

150. ke:t pa:r ökör teve: a fogatot.
        (C1   )

151.   az orsa:gu:ton ve:gig a seke:rrel
                        (B12   )

152.   a ne:gy ökör laššačka:n ballagott.
        (B1   ) (G1   )

153.*   vila:goš e:j volt. a hold fenn vala,
        (E4   )   (B12) (B3   )

154.   halva:nyan ja:rt a megsakadt felhö:kben
        (E4   )   (A5   )

155.   mike:nt a bu:š hölgy, aki fe:rjinek
        (E5   ) (B1   )

156.   ši:rhalma:t kereši a temetö:ben.
        (E4   )

157.   kalma:r sellö: ja:rt a somse:d mezö:kön,
        (E2   )   (B12   )

158.   š vett a füvektö:l e:deš illatot. (. . .)
             (B12   )

159.   a ta:ršaša:gban e:n iš ott vale:k,
                        (B3   )

160.   š vale:k somse:dja e:pen eržike:nek,
        (E3   )

161.   a ta:ršaša:gnak többi tagjai

162.   bese:lgete:nek š e:nekelgete:nek.
        (E1   )

163.   e:n a:bra:ndoztam š so:ltam eržike:hez,

164.   ne va:lassunk magunknak čillagot. (. . .)
        (C6   )
            (A7   )

165.* so:le:k e:n a:bra:ndozva eržike:hez,
    (E5)

166.   a čillag vissa fog vezetni majd
      (A7   )

167.   a mult idö:knek boldog emle:ke:hez,
      (B1   )

168.   ha elsakast a šorš egyma:što:l minket.
      (B8   )

169.   š va:lastottunk magunknak čillagot. (. . .)
      (E6   )

170.** be somoru: az e:let e:nnekem,
    (C7   )

171.   mio:ta eltemette:k kedvešem.
    (E4)

172.   čak u:gy le:zengek mint az ö:s vira:ga,
      (B3   )   (B5   )

173.   mej minden sellö: e:rkeze:šivel

174.   egy-egy megsa:radt sirmot hullat el,
      (E5) (D1   )

175.   š mej čüggedt fö:vel kimula:ša:t va:rja.

176.* a fa:jdalom gyakorta mcgrohan,
         (G1   )

177.   mint e:hezö: vad, me:rgeššilajan,
      (A6   )

178.   š e:leš körme:t sivembe va:gja me:jen.
    (E2   ) (G1   )

179. kia:ltok a šorš ellen a:tkokat,
     (E4   ) (B12)

180. amej az embernek menynyet mutat,
     (E5)   (G1   )

181. hanem megtiltja, hogy bele: ne le:pjen.
     (E5   )(D1   ) (B10   ) (C6   )

182.* legtöbbsör čendeš, ne:ma ba:natom,
     (D2   )
     (E4   )

183. e:lek. nem e:lek. sinte nem tudom.
     (F) (C6   )   (B6   )

184. jön e:š megso:li:t egy-ke:t jo:bara:tom,
           (D1   )
       (B9   )

185. bese:deikre ritka:n felelek.
     (E1   )

186. örültem egykor, hogyha jöttenek,
     (E4   )

187. mošt, hogyha mennek, si:vešebben la:tom.

188. gyakran bojongok föl-š-le ce:ltalan,
     (E3   )

189. bojongok, mi:g, azt šem tudom, hogyan,
     (E4   )   (B11   ) (E5   )

190. a dra:ga kišja:ny ši:rhalma:hoz e:rek.

191. e:deš reme:ny tart ottan engemet,
     (E2   )

192. reme:lem, hogy majd si:vem megreped. . .
     (E4   )

193.   me:rt čalnak mindig, mindig a reme:nyek.
       (C8   )   (B12   )

194.** ne fogjon šenki könynyelmü:en
       (C6   )

195.   a hu:rok pengete:šihez.

196.   nagy munka:t va:llal az maga:ra,
       (C1   )   (B8   )

197.   ki mošt keze:be lantot ves.
       (B8   )

198.   ha nem tuds ma:št, mint eldalolni
       (B6   )

199.   šaja:t fa:jdalmad š örömed,
       (E2   )

200.   ninč ra:d sükše:ge a vila:gnak,
       (C6   )   (B12   )
          (B8   )

201.   š aze:rt a sent fa:t fe:lretedd.
       (E5   ) (B1   )

202.* pusta:ban bujdošunk, mint hajdan
       (E4   )

203.   ne:pe:vel mo:zeš bujdosott,
       (E4   )

204.   š követte, mejet išten külde
       (E4   )

205.   veze:rül, a la:ngoslopot.
       (E4   ) (B12   )

206.   u:jabb idö:kben išten ijen
       (E2   )

207.   la:ngoslopoknak rendele:
        (E1   )

208.   a költö:ket, hogy ö:k veześśe:k
                   (B4   )

209.   a ne:pet ka:naa:n fele:.
                   (A4   )

210.*   elö:re ha:t mind, aki költö:,
        (E4)

211.   a ne:ppel tü:zön-vi:zen a:t.

212.   a:tok rea:, ki elhaji:tja
        (E3   )

213.   keze:bö:l a ne:p za:slaja:t,
        (E4   )(B12)

214.   a:tok rea:, ki gya:vaśa:gbo:l
        (E3   )

215.   vagy lomhaśa:gbo:l elmarad,

216.   hogy, mi:g a ne:p küzd, fa:rad, izzad,

217.   pihenjen ö: a:rnye:k alatt.
        (E4)   (G1   )

218.*   vannak hamiś pro:fe:ta:k, akik
        (H1   )

219.   azt hirdetik nagy gonosan,
        (C4   )(C1   )

220.   hogy ma:r mega:llhatunk, mert itten
                   (D1   )

221.   az i:ge:retnek földe van.

222.   hazugša:g, semtelen hazugša:g,
       (E4   ) (A5   )

223.   mit millio:k ca:folnak meg,
       (A2   )

224.   kik nap heve:ben, e:hen-somjan,
       (B5   )

225.   ke:tše:gbeešve tengenek.
       (E1   )

226.* ha majd a bö:še:g košara:bo:l

227.   mindenki egyara:nt vehet,
       (E4   ) (A1   )

228.   ha majd a jognak astala:na:l

229.   mind egyara:nt foglal hejet,
       (C8   )
                 (A1   )

230.   ha majd a sellem napvila:ga

231.   ragyog minden ha:z ablaka:n,
       (E3   )

232.   akkor mondhatjuk, hogy mega:lljunk,
       (E3   )   (D1   )
                     (B10   )

233.   mert itt van ma:r a ka:naa:n.
       (B3   )

234.* e:s addig. addig ninč megnyugva:š,
                     (B6   )

235.   addig fojva:št küsködni kell.
       (H1   )

236. tala:n az e:let munka:inke:rt
      (E5)

237. nem fog fizetni šemmivel,
      (C6   )

238. de a hala:l majd semeinket
        (B12)

239. seli:d, la:gy čo:kkal za:rja be,
      (E5) (C1   )

240. š vira:gköte:llel, šejempa:rna:n
        (E1   )

241. boča:t le a föld me:jibe.
      (E5)   (B12)

242.** magyar vagyok. legsebb orsa:g haza:m
        (E3   ) (D2)   (G2)
                        (E2   )

243. az öt vila:gre:s nagy terü:lete:n.
        (B1   ) (B1   )

244. egy kiš vila:g maga. ninč anynyi sa:m,
        (B1   )   (C6   )
        (A7   )

245. aha:ny a se:pše:g gazdag kebele:n.
      (E5   )

246. van rajta be:rc, amej tekintetet ve:t
      (C8   )   (H1   )

247. a kaspi-tenger habjain iš tu:l.

248. e:š ro:naš:ga, mintha a föld ve:ge:t
                    (B12)

249. kerešne:, ojan messe-messe nyu:l.
      (E4   )

250.* magyar vagyok. terme:setem komoj,
      (E3   ) (F   ) (G2   )

251. mint hegedü:ink elšö: hangjai,

252. ajkamra fel-felröppen a mošoj,
      (E4   )   (B12   )

253. de nevete:šem ritka:n hallani.

254. ha az öröm legjobban fešti ke:pem,
        (B12   ) (D2   )

255. magaš kedvemben ši:rva fakadok,
      (E2   )

256. de arcom vi:g a ba:nat ideje:ben,

257. mert nem akarom, hogy šajna:ljatok.
        (B6   ) (B10   )

258.* magyar vagyok. büske:n tekintek a:t
      (E3   ) (E3   )

259. a multnak tengere:n, ahol semem
                            (H1   )

260. egekbe nyu:lo: kö:sikla:kat la:t,
      (E4   )

261. nagy tetteidet, bajnok nemzetem.
      (C1   )

262. euro:pa si:npada:n mi iš ja:tsottunk,
      (E4   )   (B11   )

263.   š mienk nem volt a legkišebb serep,
       (E5   ) (C6   ) (A5   )

264.   ugy rettege: a föld kira:ntott kardunk,
       (C3   )   (D1   )

265.   mint a villa:mot e:jjel a gyerek.
       (B12   )   (B12   )

266.* magyar vagyok. mi moštan a magyar.
       (E3   ) (C8   ) (B12   )

267.   holt dičö:še:g halva:ny ki:še:rtete.
       (C1   ) (G1   )

268.   föl-föltünik š lebu:vik nagy hamar,
       (D1   ) (D1   ) (B1   )
       (E1   )

269.   ha vert az o:ra, odva me:jibe.

270.   hogy hallgatunk. a ma:šodik somse:dig
       (C8   ) (A5   )

271.   alig hogy küldjük e:letünk nese:t
       (E5)   (A3   )

272.   š šaja:t testve:rink, kik rea:nk ke:si:tik
       (E2   ) (B9   )

273.   a gya:s š gyala:zat fekete meze:t.
       (B8   ) (A5   )

274.* magyar vagyok. š arcom se:gyenben e:g,
       (E3   ) (H1   )

275.   se:gyenlenem kell, hogy magyar vagyok.
       (E1   )   (B10   )

276.   itt mina:lunk nem iš hajnallik me:g,
        (C3   ) (C6   )
                         (B11   )

277.   holott ma:šhol ma:r a nap u:gy ragyog.
        (H1   )   (B12) (B3   )

278.   de šemmi kinče:rt š hi:re:rt a vila:gon
                                   (B12   )

279.   el nem hagyna:m e:n sülö:földemet,
        (B6   )

280.   mert seretem, hö:n seretem, ima:dom
                       (C3   ) (F   )

281.   gyala:zata:ban iš nemzetemet.
        (E1   )   (G2   )

282.** me:g ke:r a ne:p, mošt adjatok neki.
                         (C8   )

283.   vagy nem tudja:tok, mij sörnyü: a ne:p
                             (B2   )

284.   ha fölkel e:š nem ke:r, de ves, ragad.
                    (C6   )   (F   )

285.   nem hallotta:tok do:ža györgy hire:t.
        (C6   ) (A3   )

286.   izzo: vaštro:non ö:t ele:gete:tek,
        (E2   )   (D1   )

287.   de selleme:t a tü:z nem e:gete: meg,
                             (C6   )

288.   mert az maga tü:z. ugy vigya:zzatok,
        (H2   ) (B3   )

289. išme:t pusti:that e la:ng rajtatok.
      (E3   ) (B12)

290.* š a ne:p hajdan čak eledelt kiva:nt,
          (H2   )   (A2   )

291. mivelhogy akkor me:g a:llat vala.
      (E4   )   (B8   )

292. de az a:llatbo:l ve:gre ember lett,
         (B12   )

293. š emberhez illik, hogy legyen joga.
      (E4   )   (B10   )

294. jogot teha:t, emberjogot a ne:pnek.
      (E3   ) (E1   )

295. mert jogtalanša:g a legru:tabb be:jeg
                        (D2   )
                        (B12   )

296. išten teremtme:nye:n, š ki ra:šüti,
      (E2   )

297. išten keze:t el nem kerü:lheti.
      (E2   ) (B6   )

298.* š mie:rt vagytok ti kiva:ltša:gosok.
      (E3   )

299. mie:rt a jog čupa:n tina:latok.
      (E5)   (H2   ) (H2   )

300. apa:itok megserze:k a haza:t,
      (E1   ) (D1   ) (B12   )

301. de ra:ja a ne:p-izzada:š čorog.
            (B12)(A2   )
              (H2   )

302. mit e:r čak ekke:p so:lni, itt a ba:nya.
    (C8   )

303. ke:z iš kell me:g, mej a földet kiha:nyja,
    (B11   )   (B12   ) (D1   )

304. ami:g föltü:nik az arany ere. . .
    (E5) (D1   ) (B12   )

305. š e ke:znek ninčen šemmi e:rdeme.

306.* š ti, kik vallja:tok ojan gö:göšen,
    (B9   )

307. mienk a haza e:š mienk a jog.
    (E5   )   (B9   )

308. haza:tokkal mit tenne:tek vajon,
    (E1   ) (C4   )

309. ha az ellenše:g ütne rajtatok. . .
    (B12   )

310. de ezt ke:rdeznem, engedelmet ke:rek,
    (B4   )

311. majd elfeledtem gyö:ri vite:zše:gtek.
    (C8   )

312. mikor emeltek ma:r emle:ksobort
    (E3   ) (B8   )

313. a šok hö:š la:bnak, mej ott u:gy futott.
    (C1   )   (B3   )

314.* jogot a ne:pnek, az emberiše:g
    (E5)   (B12   )

315. nagy sent neve:ben, adjatok jogot,
    (B1   ) (A7   )

316. š a hon neve:ben egyseršmind, amej
    (B5   )   (E5)

317. eldö:1, ha nem nyer u:j ve:doslopot.
    (D1) (B6   )(B1   )
    (E5)

318. az alkotma:ny ro:ža:ja a tie:tek,
    (A3   )(B12   )

319. tövi:šeit a ne:p köze: vete:tek.
    (E1) (B7   )
        (A1   )

320. ide a ro:ža ne:ha:ny levele:t
    (E5)

321. š vegye:tek vissa a töviš fele:t. (. . .)
    (E4   )   (B12   )

322.** föl tudna:m e:n iš öltöztetni
    (C8   )

323. se:p ri:m-š-me:rte:kbe versemet,
    (C1   )

324. amint illö: megla:togatni
    (H1   )(D1   )

325. a ta:ršaša:gi termeket.

326.* de esme:im nem henye ifjak,
        (C6   )

327. kik e:lnek, hogy mulaššanak,
        (B10   )

328. hogy felfürtözve, kestyü:š ke:zzel

329. la:togato:ba ja:rjanak.
(E1   )

330.* nem čeng a kard, nem dörg az a:gyu:,
(C6   )   (C6   )

331. a rožda-a:lom lepte meg.

332. de tart a harc, a kard š az a:gyu:

333. hejett most esme:k küzdenek.
(E5   )

334.* ott a:llok e:n is a čata:ban
(C3   )   (B12   )

335. katona:id közt, sa:zadom.
(E1   )

336. čata:zok veršeimmel, egy-egy
(E4   )

337. harcoš lege:ny minden dalom.
(E2   ) (G1   )

338.* rongyoš lege:nyek, de vite:zek,
(E2   ) (B9   )

339. mind ba:tran harcol, ba:tran va:g,
(C8   )

340. š a katona:nak ba:torša:ga

341. tesi di:se:t, nem a ruha:k.
(H1   ) (C6   )
(B12   )

342.* š nem ke:rdem e:n, hogy költeme:nyim
(C6   )

343. tu:le:lnek-e majd engemet.
      (D1   )
      (E1   )

344. ha el kell ešniök tala:n e
          (A7   )

345. čata:ban, a:m hadd eššenek.
      (E4   )   (C7   )

346.* me:g akkor iš sent les e könyv, hol
          (B11   )

347. meghalt esme:im nyugsanak,
      (D1   )
      (E2   )

348. mert hö:šök temetö:je az, kik

349. a sabadša:ge:rt haltanak.

350.** ne ba:ntšon az meg, fe:nyeš napvila:gom,
       (C6   )

351. ha arcom ne:ha elšöte:tedik.

352. nem lehetek e:n, ba:rmike:nt kiva:nom,
      (C6   )   (A1   )

353. me:g elö:tted šem fojton-fojva vig.

354.* nyugtaššon meg, hogy ijenkor sivembe
      (E4   )   (A7   )

355. a ba:natot nem te hoza:d vala,
              (C6   )
                  (B4   )

356. hogyan serezne:l ba:natot nekem te,
      (E3   )

357.   a földnek e:gnek legjobb angyala.

358.* ege:sen ma:š az, ame:rt engem ne:ha
       (E4   )

359.   kiše:rteteš halva:nyša:g si:ne fed,
       (E6   )

360.   e:n egy sellemnek vagyok martale:ka,
         (B9   )

361.   mej meg-megla:togatni nem feled.
                      (B6   )

362.* hia:ba ke:rem, hastalan ešengek,
       (E4   )   (A1   )

363.   hogy hagyjon el, hagyjon magamra ma:r.
                      (E3   )

364.   ke:rlelhetetlen, šiket ö:. nem enged,
       (E1   )   (C6   )

365.   tala:n örökke: vissa-vissaja:r.
       (H1   )

366.* šoksor, midö:n a ke:j lege:dešb nedve
       (E5   ) (E5   )   (D2   )

367.   e:rinti ma:r-ma:r somjaš ajkamat,
       (E4   )

368.   megjelenik, kezem mega:ll ijedve
       (D1   )   (D1   ) (G2   )
       (E1   ) (E3   )

369.   e:š földre ejti a telt poharat.
                  (B12)
                     (C1   )

370.* e sellem a mult. mult idö:m emle:ke,
        (B12) (B1   )
              (A3   )

371.   a legvadabb, legborzasto:bb alak,
        (D2   )
        (A5   )

372.   mit egy pokoli bor heve:tö:l e:gve
        (B9   ) (B5   )

373.   a šorš visa:ji kigondoltanak.
        (B5   )

374.* ezen sellemnek vagyok odavetve.
        (E2   )

375.   fel-feltör hozza:m ši:rja me:jibül,
        (D1   )
        (E4   )

376.   š mi:g šu:gja re:meš ige:it fülembe,
                        (A7   )

377.   lelkem lelketlen sikla:va: kövül.
        (H1   ) (A2   )

378.   ne so:li:tš ekkor, u:gyšem e:rtene:lek,
        (C6   )

379.   e:deš hangod šem hatna si:vemig.
        (E2   )

380.   va:rd el be:ke:ben, mi:g a jelene:šnek
        (H1   )

381.   irto:ztato: o:ra:ja eltelik.
        (E6   )

382.*   körü:lem ijen a:lom fon hideg kart,
        (E4   )   (G2)

383.   š miatta megiš menynyi a kinom.
        (E4   )   (B12   )

384.   a:lom čupa:n, de mit hasna:l. amig tart,
        (H2   )   (B4   ) (F   )

385.   esembe nem jut, hogy čak a:lmodom.
        (E4   ) (B6   )

386.** bese:l a fa:kkal a bu:š ö:si se:l,
        (E5)   (B12)

387.   halkan bese:lget, nem hallhatni meg.
        (E3   ) (B6   )

388.   vajon mit mond nekik. bese:dire
        (E5) (C4   ) (F   )

389.   a fa:k merengve ra:zza:k fejöket.
        (B8   )

390.   de:l š ešt között van az idö:, nyujto:zom
        (C8   )   (B12) (F   )

391.   a pamlagon ve:gig ke:nyelmešen,
                  (G2)(G2   )

392.   keblemre hajtva feječke:je:t, alsik
        (E4   )

393.   kis feleše:gem me:jen, čendesen.
        (C1   )

394.*   egyik kezemben e:deš sendergö:m
        (E2   )

395.   seli:deden hulla:mzo: kebele,
        (E6   )

396.   ma:šik kezemben imakönyvem, a
        (E2   )

397.   sabadša:gha:boru:k törte:nete.
        (E1   )
               (A3   )

398.   minden betü:je üštököščillagke:nt
        (E2   )

399.   nyargal kerestül magaš lelkemen (. . .)
        (E3   )

400.*   arany čal s oštor kerget te:gedet
        (E5)

401.   a žamoke:rt megvi:ni, solgane:p,
                     (D1   )

402.   e:š a sabadša:g. egyet mošojog,
        (B12   )

403.   š mind, aki hi:ve, a harcte:rre le:p,
                     (B12   )

404.   š e:rette, mint a se:p ja:nyto:l vira:got,
           (E4)   (B1   )
                         (A7   )

405.   šebet, hala:lt oj jo:kedvvel vesen (. . .)
        (E5)(E5   )(C2   )
                     (A1   )

406.*   ha:ny dra:ga e:let hullt ma:r e:rted el,
        (C8   )

407. oh sent sabadša:g. e:š mi hasna van.
    (C7   )   (C8   )
      (B1   )

408. de les, ha ninč. tie:d a diadal
          (E5)

409. majd a čata:knak uto:so:iban,
      (B12   )

410. š halottaide:rt bossut is fogs a:llni,
      (E1   )

411. š a bossua:lla:š rettentö: lesen (. . .)
         (A1   )

412.* ve:rpanora:ma leng elö:ttem el,
      (E1   )   (H2   )

413. a jövendö: kor jelene:šei,
      (A6   )

414. šaja:t ve:rök tava:ba fu:lnak be:
      (E2   )

415. a sabadša:gnak ellenše:gei.

416. egy kis menynydörge:š si:vem doboga:ša,
      (B1   )

417. š villa:mok, futnak a:ltal fejemen, (. . .)
      (E4   )

418.** ele:g šoka: voltunk fajanko:k,
      (H1   )(H2   )

419. legyünk ve:gte:re katona:k.
     (E3   )

420.   ele:g volt ma:r a furuja:bo:l,
        (E5)

421.   riadjatok meg, haršona:k.
        (E1   )

422.*   elö:l pofoznak, ha:tul ru:gnak,
        (H1   )

423.   haza:m, tova:bb iš tü:rs-e me:g.
        (E5   ) (E5   )

424.   nem lobbans föl, mi:g menynyköve:vel
        (C6   )

425.   föl nem gyu:jt a haragoš e:g.
        (B6   ) (B12   )

426.*   oh nemzetem, ha:t bi:rnak te:ged
        (C7   )

427.   örökke: fe:ken tartani
        (E4   )

428.   a nagyfejü:ek s kiššivü:ek,

429.   a ta:blabi:ra:k savai.

430.*   vagy u:gy van, amint ö:k bese:lik,
            (B3   )   (B4   )

431.   hogy elfajult ma:r a magyar,
                            (B12   )

432.   hogy gyöngeše:gbö:l, gya:vaša:gbo:l

433.   harcolni nem bi:r, nem akar.
        (E4   ) (B6   ) (B6   )

434.* hazugša:g, senynyeš gaz hazugša:g
       (E4   )   (B1   )

435.   š mint a nyelvetek, akkora.
           (B12   )

436.   nem pežg, nem habzik a magyar ne:p,
       (C6   ) (C6   ) (B12   )

437.   čendeš, de tüzeš, mint bora.
       (E5   )   (B9   )

438.* čak volna harc, čak öntene:k ma:r

439.   ve:rünket, ba:rčak öntene:k.
       (E4   )

440.   majd megla:tja:tok, holtre:seg les

441.   minden čepptö:l az ellenše:g
       (E2   )

442.* šiešš, haza:m, napfe:nyre hozni
       (F   )

443.   vila:graso:lo: hi:redet,
       (E1   )

444.   mit ne:met ja:rom, ne:met a:rma:ny

445.   elrablott e:š eltemetett.
       (D1   )   (D1   )

446.* jö:jjön ki kardod a hüvejbö:l,
       (E5)   (B12   )

447.   mint fellegek közü:l a nap,
           (A4   )

448.   vaku:ljanak meg š megvaku:lnak,
        (E1   )

449.   akik rea:pillantanak. (...)
        (H1   )

450.** respublika, sabadša:g gyermeke
        (E1   ) (E4   )

451.   š sabadša:g anyja, vila:g jo:tevö:je,
        (E4   )

452.   ki bujdošol, mint a ra:ko:ciak,
                          (B12   )

453.   kösöntelek a ta:volbo:l elö:re.
        (E1   ) (A7   )

454.*   mošt ho:dolok, midö:n me:g messe vagy,
        (C8   ) (E5   )

455.   midö:n me:g re:meš a:tkozott neved van,
        (E5   )   (A5   )

456.   midö:n me:g, aki megfesi:teni
        (E5   )

457.   ke:s te:gedet, azt bečülik legjobban.
                       (C4   ) (D2   )

458.*   mošt ho:dolok, mošt üdvözöllek e:n,
        (C8   ) (C8   )

459.   his akkor u:gyiš ho:dolo:d ele:g les,
                          (A7   )

460.   ha a magašbo:l ellenidre majd
        (B12   )

461.   a ve:reš porba diadallal ne:zes.

462.* mert gyö:zni fogs, dičö: respublika,
                    (E2   )

463.   ba:r veššen e:g e:š föld ele:dbe ga:tot,
                    (A7   )

464.   mike:nt egy u:j, de sent napo:leon
       (E5   )   (B1   )

465.   elfoglalod majd a kerek vila:got.
       (D1   )   (B12   )
       (E1   )

466.* kit meg nem te:ri:t se:p seli:d semed,
                    (C6   )(B1   )

467.   hol a seretet olta:rla:ngja čillog,
            (B12   )

468.   majd megte:ri:ti azt silaj kezed,
                    (B8   )

469.   mejben hala:loš ve:snek kardja villog.
       (H1   )

470.* te le:s a gyö:zö:, a diadal-i:v
       (C4   )   (B12   )

471.   ha elke:sü:l, a te sa:modra le:sen,
                    (B4   )

472.   aka:r vira:goš tarka pa:žiton,
       (H1   )

473.   aka:r a ve:rnek vöröš tengere:ben
       (E5)

474.*   seretne:m tudni, ott lesek-e e:n
        (E4   )   (B3   )

475.   a gyö:zedelmi fe:nyeš ünnepe:jen.

476.   vagy akkora:ra ma:ṛ ta:n elvis az

477.   enye:set š ott lenn tart a ši:rba me:jen.
        (E4   ) (B3   )

478.*   ha meg nem e:rem e nagy ünnepet,
        (C6   )(B12)

479.   bara:tim, emle:kezzetek meg ro:lam,
        (E4   )

480.   republika:nuš vagyok š az lesek
        (E1   )   (B4   )

481.   a föld alatt iš ott a koporšo:ban.
        (B7   )

482.*   jertek ki hazza:m, š ott kia:ltšatok
        (E5   )   (B3   )

483.   širomna:l e:ljent a respublika:ra,
        (E4   )   (B12   )

484.   meghallom e:n azt, š akkor be:ke sa:ll
        (D1   )
        (E4   )

485.   ez üldözött, e fa:jo: si:v pora:ra.
                            (B5   )

486.** tudod, midö:n elö:sör ültünk
        (F   ) (H1   )

487.   e to: fölött, e fa:k alatt.
        (B7   ) (B7   )

488.   röpü:l a gyorš idö: fölöttünk,
        (E5) (B1   )
                (A7   )

489.   azo:ta ke:t e:v elhaladt.
        (E4) (B1   )

490.*   ij ö:s volt akkor iš, ijen se:p
        (C2)   (F   )

491.   mošojgo: ö:si de:luta:n,
        (E4   )

492.   seli:d fuvalmak i:gy rezgette:k
        (E2   ) (B3   )

493.   a ša:rga lombokat a fa:n.

494.*   igy tükröze: vissa a to:nak
        (C3   ) (H2)

495.   vize a tista ke:k eget,
        (E5)   (B1   )

496.   igy ringato:zott ama čo:nak
        (C3   )

497.   a:bra:ndošan a vi:z felett.
        (E1   ) (B7   )

498.*   de akkor me:g čak gondolatban

499.   e:lveztem menynyorsa:gomat,
        (E4   )

500.   mert akkor me:g nem čo:kolhattam,
                    (C6   )

501.   mint moštan, e:deš ajkadat.

502.*   ke:t e:ve annak. šokat elvitt
        (C1   )

503.   az idö: tö:lem azalatt,

504.   de nem panaslok, mert amenynyit
        (B6   )(B9   )

505.   elvitt, šokkal többet hozott.
        (D1)(H1   )
        (E5)

506.*   te:ged hozott meg nekem, te:ged,
        (E3   )

507.   reme:nyim fe:nyeš gyöngyšora,
        (E4   )

508.   kie:rt az örök üdvöšše:get
        (E5)

509.   ezerser adna:m e:n oda.
        (E4)(A7   )

510.*   maradjunk me:g itt, le:gy mellettem,
        (E4   )   (B7   )

511.   hol u:gy bušu:ltam egykoron,
        (B3   )

512.   hagyj engem itt mošt elmerengnem
        (C8   )

513.   ve:getlen boldogša:gomon.
        (E4   )

514.** ti aka:cfa:k a kertben,

515.   ti se:pemle:kü fa:k,

516.   amejeken sivemnek
     (H1   )

517.   oj dra:ga minden a:g,
     (C2   )

518.* kedveš fa:k, üdvezelve
     (E5)

519.   e:š a:ldva legyetek,

520.   a:ldom me:g azt iš, aki
     (E5)

521.   titeket ültetett.
     (E4)

522.* harmatnak š napšuga:rnak
     (E4   )

523.   a:lda:ša rajtatok,
     (E4)

524.   vida:m dalošmada:rto:l
     (E2   )

525.   reskeššen a:gatok.
     (E4)

526.* örök tavas lakozze:k
     (E2   )

527.   zöld fürteiteken,
     (C1   )

528.   hogy e:ltetek, mike:nt az
           (E5   )

529.   enye:m, oj se:p legyen.
       (E5   ) (C2   )
                 (B3   )

530.* itt la:ttam e:n elö:sör
       (C3   ) (B9   )

531.   kedveš galambomat,
       (E2   )

532.   itt la:ttam ö:t elö:sör
       (C3   ) (B9   )

533.   ez aka:cfa:k alatt.
       (A4   )

534.* itt ü:lt e lombok alja:n
       (C3   )

535.   itt ü:lt semközt velem,
       (C3

536.   itten röpült seme:bö:l
       (E3   )

537.   sivembe serelem.
       (E4   )

538.* tudom me:g, hogyne tudna:m,
       (E5   )

539.   haba:r re:gen vala,
       (H1   )

540.   az o:ra:t, hol kigyu:ladt
                    (D1   )
                 (B9   )

541.   serelmem hajnala.
       (E4   )

542.* ez volt a hajnal. ijen
       (C4   )

543.   nem e:keši:te me:g
       (C6   )

544.   te:ged, te ve:ghetetlen,
       (E5   )

545.   te re:gteremtett e:g.

546.* letü:nt imma:r e hajnal
       (D1   )
       (E3   )

547.   mege:rtem a delet,
       (D1   ) (B12)
       (E4   )

548.   š ez ta:n nem oj rege:nyeš,
              (C6   )
                   (B2   )

549.   de šokkal melegebb.

550.* mikor jön majd az alkony,
       (E5   )

551.   serelmem alkonya.
       (E4   )

552.   ettö:l ne fe:lj, sivcmnck
       (E5) (C6   ) (F   )

553.   ima:dott assonya.
       (E4   )

554.* eljö: ez iš, de ke:šön,
       (D1) (B11)
       (E5)

555.   aze:rt jö: majd, ha jö:,
       (E5)

556.   hogy le:gyen arcainkon

557.   se:p arany semfedö:.
       (C1   )

558.* ǯ a földbe, ha letesnek,
              (D1   )
              (B9   )

559.   majd čillag ke:piben

560.   ragyog le zöld ǯirunkra
       (E5) (B1   )

561.   ǯöte:tke:k e:jeken.
       (E4   )

562.** euro:pa čendeǯ, ujra čendeǯ,
       (E4   )

563.   elzu:gtak forradalmai.
       (D1   )
       (E4   )

564.   se:gyen rea:. lečendeǯü:lt e:ǯ
       (E3   ) (D1   )

565.   sabadǯa:ga:t nem vi:vta ki.
       (E1   ) (C6   )

566.* maga:ra hagyta:k, egy-maga:ra
       (E4)

567.   a gya:va ne:pek a magyart.
                   (B12   )

568. la:nc čörg minden ke:zen, čupa:n a
          (G1   ) (F   )

569. magyar keze:ben čeng a kard.
      (E2   )

570.* de ha:t ke:tše:gbe kell-e ešnünk,
      (B9   )

571. ha:t bu:šuljunk-e e-miatt.

572. ellenkezö:leg, oh hon, inka:bb
      (E1   )

573. ez le:gyen, ami lelket ad.
      (C4   )

574.* emelje ez föl lelkeinket,
      (E4   )

575. hogy mi vagyunk a la:mpafe:ny,
          (B4   )

576. mej amidö:n a többi alsik,

577. e:g a šöte:tše:g e:jjele:n.
      (B12   )

578.* ha a mi fe:nyünk nem lobogna
          (B12)   (B6   )

579. a ve:ghetetlen e:jen a:t,

580. azt gondolhatna:k fönn az e:gben,
      (C4   )

581. hogy elenye:sett a vila:g.
              (B12   )

582.*   tekintš rea:nk, tekintš, sabadša:g,
        (E3   ) (F   )

583.   išmerd meg moštan ne:pedet,
        (E5)

584.   midö:n ma:š könynyet šem mer adni,
        (E5)

585.   mi ve:rrel a:ldozunk neked.
        (A4   )

586.*   vagy kell-e me:g több, hogy a:lda:šod
                         (B10   )

587.   nem e:rdemetlen sa:lljon ra:nk.
        (C6   )

588.   e hü:tlen korban mi uto:šo:
                     (B8   )

589.   egyetlen hi:veid vala:nk.
        (E4   ) (A2   )

TRANSLATION OF THE TEXT

adorned by golden wheat, thou plains
upon which light mirage
flirtingly plays fairy games,
remember me? oh recognize thy son!
5.   it was long ago, true, when under these poplar trees
in the shadow I last had a rest,
over my head while through autumn's air
your migrating cranes' letter V was flying;
while at the threshold of the ancient house
10.   farewell's broken voice I whispered;
and the good mother's last word of blessing
the winds have long since swept away.
since then many years have been born,
and many years have passed away,
15.   and riding changing fortune's chariot
the wide world I have roamed all over.
the world is life's school;
of my sweat it had demanded much,
for so jerky, so hard is the road,
20.   one travels across so many deserts.
this I know, like no one else knows,
to whom its misfortunes experience
out of a dark glass has so often offered,
that I had rather drunk death!
25.   but now gloom, the long agony,
of which my heart has so often swollen,
and the memory of all misery
are all washed away by tears of a sacred joy;
for where in the tender lap of my soft cradle
30.   mother milk's honey I tasted,
your gay sun is smiling at me again,
onto your faithful child, my dear fatherland!

yours am I, yours, my land,
this heart, this soul;
35.   whom would I love if you
it were not that I love?
my heart's innermost is a holy church,
its altar is your picture.
let you stand, and if I must, the temple
40.   I will shatter for you;
and the broken heart's
last prayer,
blessing onto the fatherland, my god's
blessing onto it!
45.   but I am not telling anyone,
I am not announcing,
the dearest to me that you are
in the entire world.
I secretly follow your steps,
50.   and steadfastly ever;
not like his shadow the traveller,
only in good weather.
but like twilight, growing, when
the night is near,
55.   growing is my despair when it gets dark,
my land, above you.
and I will join in where your disciples
raising their glasses
beg fate for a new light
60.   onto your sacred life;
and I will empty to the last drop the wine
of the filled bottle,
though it is bitter. . . for my tears
drop into it!

65.   one year is digging the grave of another,
they're killing each other like men.
time, just one more flutter of your wing,
and the present year too will slumber in its grave.
blow out, dying one, with your wilted lips'
70.   breath your life's candle,
I shall not register you

where my happy years are recorded.
into this head glowing with high plans
the seeds of so many noble thoughts have you planted,
75.   and I their abundant fruits
observing, look at them proudly.
as an award for my not lazy labor
the star of fame has cast its rays upon me,
and yet I will not register you, (. . .)
80.   my heart for long in destiny's left hand
painful sorrow's burning world used to be;
you, ageing year, warned that it not burn,
and by your appeal the wild flame ceased.
extinguished cinder is left of my sorrow only
85.   over the ruined and half-sound heart; (. . .)
oh dying year! at your grave's side, me
hope is rocking in its soft cradle,
and if I should what it prophesies believe,
at heaven's threshold am I standing.
90.   in the proximity of such a joyous time
am I saying, fading year, farewell to you, (. . .)
cast upon you, imploring desperately,
are glassy eyes of my sighing nation,
and you its sighs failing to acknowledge
95.   thus answered thundering, no!
you have torn up my nation's wreath
that its youthful hope has placed upon its head,
that's why I will not register you, (. . .)

where have you gone? you of my better hopes'
100.   morning star, so soon burned away!
I will seek you; am I seeking you in vain?
or shall we see each other again?
when in the quiet midst of night
its pale shine the moon onto the earth directs,
105.   the graveyard's threshold I will step across,
and bow my head over your grave.
will you then wake up from your dreams,
and leave your deep, cool cushion?
that you hear what my lips say,
110.   love's imploring word. (. . .)

that you wipe from my tired eyelashes
the tears showering for you. (. . .)
that your spirit from my burning kisses
and my heart's fire borrow warmth.
115. or will their dead the graves refuse to yield
and only in heaven will you meet me?
or will neither the night nor heaven ever
show you to me again?

someone has murdered himself,
120. that's what has brought this ugly weather.
the wind blowing, the disk dancing
in front of the barbershops.
where is happiness nowadays?
in a cozy warm room.
125. the farm hand and his woman
are sawing and splitting wood;
their child, wrapped in a colorful blanket,
is bent to out-scream the windstorm. (. . .)
walking with long steps up and down
130. is the soldier at his post;
he is counting his steps,
for in his pain what else can he do? (. . .)
the long-legged peddler
is carrying his worn-out stuff;
135. his nose is ripe pepper,
and from the cold his tears are running. (. . .)
walking on the road is the travelling actor
from one village to the next;
warm clothing he has none,
140. but nevertheless he is starved. (. . .)
and the gypsy? his teeth chattering
under the ragged tents;
the wind is knocking and entering,
though the gypsy hasn't said, come in! (. . .)

145. what you'll hear didn't happen in budapest.
there such romantic things don't happen.
the gentlemen and women of the company
got on a wagon and travelled thereupon.

they went on a wagon, but an ox-drawn wagon.
150. two pairs of oxen made up the harness.
along the highway drawing the wagon
the four oxen took step after step.
it was a bright night. the moon was out,
moving pale amongst the broken clouds,
155. like an unhappy lady who her husband's grave
tries to find in the cemetery.
light wind whispered across the neighboring meadows
and took sweet fragrance from the grasses. (. . .)
I happened to be in the company myself,
160. and happened to sit next to betsy.
other members of the company
were chatting and singing.
I day-dreamed and said to betsy,
shall we choose a star for ourselves? (. . .)
165. so I spoke to betsy, day-dreaming,
the star will lead us back some time
to happy memories of the past,
when our fate will separate us from one another.
and we chose a star for ourselves. (. . .)

170. how sad life is for me, (and has been)
since the burial of my sweetheart!
I am so fragile like autumn's flower
which, with the arrival of every breeze,
lets loose a dried petal,
175. and which with its head hanging its extinction expects.
sorrowful pain often attacks me,
like a starving beast, raging,
and it cuts its sharp claws into my heart deep.
I shout curses against destiny
180. which shows heaven to man,
but forbids that he enter.
mostly quiet, silent is my sorrow;
am I alive? am I not? I almost do not know.
some good friends stop by and speak to me,
185. to their talk I rarely respond.
I was happy once if they came,
now, when they leave, I am happier.

I often roam up and down aimlessly,
I roam until —I don't even know how—
190.   to the dear maiden's grave I arrive.
sweet hope keeps me there;
I hope that my heart will break. . .
why do they deceive me always, always, those hopes!

let no one hastily begin
195.   plucking the strings!
a difficult task does he take upon himself
who now takes a harp in his hands.
if you cannot do better than to sing about
your own sorrows and joys,
200.   the world does not need you,
and therefore set aside the sacred wood.
we are hiding in the desert, like long ago
with his people moses was hiding,
and followed, which god sent
205.   for guidance, the column of flame.
in recent times god such
flame columns has ordered
poets to be, so that they lead
the people toward the promised land.
210.   forward then, all who are poets,
with the people through fire and water!
let him be cursed who casts away
from his hand the people's flag,
let him be cursed who out of cowardice
215.   or of laziness stays behind,
that, while the people struggle, tire, sweat,
he can rest in the shade.
there are false prophets who
teach unscrupulously
220.   that now we can stop, for here
is the promised land.
it is a lie, an impertinent lie
which millions disprove
who, in the heat of the sun, hungry and thirsty,
225.   desperately carry on.
when from the basket of plenty

everyone gets his equal share,
when at the table of human rights
all take their seats equally,
230.   when the bright light of spirit
shines through the window of every house,
then we can say that we can stop,
for canaan is here!
and till then? till then there is no stopping,
235.   till then one must constantly struggle.
perhaps life for our labor
will not pay anything.
but death will our eyes
with a tender, soft kiss close,
240.   and will by a flowered rope, on a silky pillow
lower us into the depth of the earth.

I am magyar. the prettiest land anywhere is my homeland
over the vast expanse of the five continents.
a little world in itself. there are fewer numbers
245.   than beauties in its rich domain.
it has mountains which look
beyond the surfs of the caspian sea,
and its plain, as if it for the world's end
would reach, so far does it extend.
250.   I am magyar. my disposition is serious,
like our violin's first sounds.
my lips may assume a smile,
but my laughter you will rarely hear.
when joy best colors my face,
255.   in my high mood I break into tears,
but my face is gay in times of sorrow,
for I don't want you to feel sorry for me.
I am magyar. I proudly survey
the sea of past ages where my eyes
260.   see cliffs reaching into the sky,
your great deeds, my champion nation.
on europe's stage we too have played,
and ours was not the smallest role;
so afraid was the world of our pulled sword
265.   like a child of lightning at night.

I am magyar. what is now the magyar?
dead glory's pale ghost.
it emerges and then disappears in a hurry
when the clock has struck, in its den's depth.
270.   how dumb we are! to the second neighbor
we barely send a sign of being alive.
and it is our own brothers now preparing for us
the black garment of mourning and shame.
I am magyar. and my face is burning of shame,
275.   I must be ashamed that I am magyar!
here at us it is not even dawning,
whereas elsewhere the sun is already so bright.
but for no treasure or reknown in the world
would I leave my land of birth,
280.   for I love, passionately love, adore,
even in its shame, my nation.

the people are still requesting, give them now!
or don't you know how terrible are the people
when they rise and do not beg but take and grab?
285.   have you not heard of györgy dózsa?
on a glowing iron throne you burned him,
but his spirit the flames did not consume,
for it is itself fire; be careful,
for this flame may devastate among you once again!
290.   long ago the people had need only of food,
since, at that time, they were still animals.
but the animals have turned human at last,
and man expects that he have rights.
rights, then, human rights for the people!
295.   for being without rights is the ugliest stamp
on god's creature, and the tatooer
god's hand cannot avoid.
and why are you the privileged ones?
why do all the rights belong to you?
300.   your fathers acquired the homeland,
but it is watered by the sweat of the common folk.
what is the use of saying, here is the mine!
you need hands too that will dig into the earth
until the vein of gold emerges. . .

305.   and these hands have no merit whatever?
         and you, who maintain so proudly,
         ours is the land and ours are the rights!
         what would you do with your homeland
         if the enemy should attack you?
310.   but I beg your pardon for asking this,
         I almost forgot your heroism at györ.
         when is it that you will build a monument
         in memory of the many brave legs that ran so fast there?
         rights for the people, in humanity's
315.   great sacred name, give rights,
         and on the nation's behalf also which
         will fall unless it gains a new column for support.
         the rose of the constitution is yours,
         its thorns you have thrown among the people.
320.   here with a few leaves of the rose,
         and take back half of the thorns!

         I too could dress into
         pretty rhyme and meter my verse,
         as it is proper to visit
325.   halls at social occasions.
         but my principles are not idle youngsters
         who live in order to live it up,
         so that ornamented, gloves in hands
         they can pay visits.
330.   no swords are clashing, no cannons are thundering,
         rusty dreams are keeping them asleep.
         but the fight is on. . . instead of sword and gun
         now principles are at battle.
         there I stand in the battle myself
335.   among your soldiers, my company!
         I shoot with my poems. . . a
         fighting fellow is every one of my songs.
         ragged fellows, but brave,
         they all fight bravely, cut bravely,
340.   and a soldier's bravery
         is his distinguishing mark, not his dress.
         I am not asking whether my poems
         will survive me?

345.
> if they must fall perhaps in this
> battle, so let them fall.
> even then sacred will be this book where
> my dead ideals lie,
> for it is a cemetery of heroes who
> have fallen for freedom.

350.
> don't let it hurt you, my bright sunshine
> if sometimes my face darkens.
> I cannot be, no matter how I wish,
> even for your sake constantly gay.
> let it console you that at such times my heart's

355.
> sadness was not caused by you. . .
> how could sorrow come from you,
> world's and heaven's best angel?
> something else it is why at times I am
> colored with ghostly paleness,

360.
> I am at the mercy of a spirit
> which never forgets to keep visiting me.
> I beg him in vain, no use to implore,
> that he leave me, leave me alone at last;
> implacable, deaf is he! he won't yield,

365.
> perhaps he will keep returning forever.
> often, when pleasure's sweetest juice
> almost touches my thirsty lips,
> he appears. . . my hands stop frightened
> and drop the filled glass.

370.
> this spirit is the past! the memory of my past,
> the wildest, most terrible figure,
> which, burned by the heat of a hellish wine,
> the strifes of fate could design.
> at the disposal of this spirit am I;

375.
> he keeps ascending to me from its deep grave,
> and while it is whispering its horrible message into my ears,
> my soul turns into a soulless rock.
> don't speak to me then, I wouldn't understand you,
> even your sweet voice would not penetrate my heart.

380.
> wait in peace until the apparition's
> terrible hour is gone.
> such a dream wraps cold arms around me,

and how great is my pain on its account!
only a dream. . . but what's the difference? while it lasts
385.   it does not occur to me that I am only dreaming.

chatting with the trees is the sad autumn wind,
chatting softly, not to be heard.
what could it tell them? in reply
the trees are shaking their heads, musing.
390.   between noon and evening is the time, I am stretching
along the sofa, comfortably. . .
laying her little head onto my bosom, asleep
is my little wife, deep and quiet.
in one hand I have my dear slumberer's
395.   gently waving breast,
in the other is my book of prayer, the
history of wars for liberty.
its every letter like a comet
dashes through my high soul. . . (. . .)
400.   gold tempts and whip chases you
to fight for the tyrant, slaves;
and liberty? it gives a smile,
and all that long for it step on the battlefield,
and for its sake, like flowers from a fair maiden,
405.   wounds and death they take cheerfully. . . (. . .)
how many dear lives have already fallen for you,
oh sacred freedom! and what's the use?
but there will be, if there isn't now; victory is yours
in the last ones of the battles,
410.   and for your dead you will take revenge,
and the revenge will be terrible!. . . (. . .)
I see a panorama of blood before me,
apparitions of the future,
in ponds of their own blood will be drowned
415.   enemies of liberty!
a little thunder is my heart's throbbing,
and lightning flashes through my head, (. . .)

we have been blockheads long enough,
let us now be soldiers!
420.   enough of the flutes,

now let the trumpets sound!
slapped in the front, kicked in the back,
my country, how long will you tolerate?
will you not explode till with its giant meteors
425.   the angry sky will set you afire?
oh my nation, so they can
hold you down forever,
the bull-headed and small-hearted,
the petty officials — by words?
430.   or is it the way they say,
that the magyar race has degenerated,
that out of weakness, cowardice
to fight it is unable, unwilling?
it is a lie, a dirty evil lie,
435.   as big as your tongue;
neither fizzing nor foaming, the magyars
are quiet, but fiery like their wine.
only if there were fight, only if finally they would shed
our blood, only if they'd shed it!
440.   you will see, dead drunk will
every drop make the enemy.
hurry, my land, and bring to light
your world-wide fame,
which german yoke, german trickery
445.   has taken and buried.
let your sword come out of the scabbard
like the sun from among the clouds,
let them be blind, and they will be blind
who take a glance at it.

450.   republic, child of liberty
and mother of liberty, helper of the world
who are hiding like the rakoczi's,
I welcome you from the distance, in advance!
I am paying tribute now while you are still far away,
455.   while your name is still terrible and cursed,
while still who to crucify you
are ready, those are respected most.
I pay tributes now, I greet you now,
for then you will have admirers plenty

460.   when from high above at your enemy
            in the bloody dust you will triumphantly daze.
            for you will be the winner, glorious republic,
            though let heaven and earth block your way,
            like a new but sacred napoleon
465.   you will conquer the entire world.
            whomever your beautious tender eyes fail to convert,
            where love's altar-flame sparkles,
            will be converted by your tough hand
            in which the sword of deadly danger flashes.
470.   you shall be the victor, the arch of triumph,
            when built, will stand for you,
            whether on a colorful flowery lawn
            or in a red sea of blood.
            I wish I knew if I will be there
475.   at the bright celebration of triumph?
            or perhaps by then I will have been taken by
            life's twilight and kept down there deep in the grave?
            should I not see this grand holiday,
            friends, remember me. . .
480.   I am republican and will be
            even under the earth in the coffin!
            come out to me and shout there
            at my grave 'hurrah' for the republic,
            it will reach my ears, and then peace will descend
485.   upon the dust of this harassed and hurting heart.

            you know, while we first sat
            above the lake, under these trees?
            fast time is flying above us,
            since then two years have been gone.
490.   it was such autumn then too, such beautiful
            smiling autumn afternoon,
            soft breezes were shaking the same way
            the yellow limbs of the tree.
            it was just like this reflection by the lake's
495.   water of the clear blue sky,
            so was that boat rocking
            dreamily over the water.
            but then only in thoughts

did I enjoy my heaven,
500.   since then I could not yet kiss,
like now, your sweet lips.
two years since. . . much has
time taken from me since,
but no complaining, for what
505.   I've lost, much more have I received.
I have received you, you,
bright pearl of my hopes,
for whom eternal redemption
I'd sacrifice a thousand times.
510.   let us stay here a while, be next to me,
where once I was so sad,
let me now lose myself in thinking about
my boundless happiness!

you acacias in the garden,
515.   you trees of beautiful memories,
on which to my heart
so dear is every branch,
dear trees, welcome
and blessed be,
520.   I am blessing even the one who
planted you.
dew's and sunshine's
blessing upon you,
let happy birds of song
525.   make your limbs tremble.
let eternal spring dwell
upon your green leaves,
that your life, like my own,
so beautiful may be.
530.   this is where I first saw
my dear sweetheart,
this is where I first saw her
under these acacias.
here under these limbs she sat,
535.   here she sat facing me,
here did from her eyes fly
love into my heart.

I still remember, how could I forget?
though it was long ago,
540.   the hour when set afire
was my love's rising sun.
this was some dawn! a kind
that had never yet adorned
you, you limitless,
545.   you long ago-created sky.
the dawn now is gone,
I have reached life's noon,
this perhaps is not so romantic
but a great deal more intimate.
550.   when is twilight to come?
my love's twilight?
of this do not be afraid, my heart's
cherished woman!
that will be here too, but late,
555.   that's why it will come, if it does,
so that there be over our faces
a nice golden veil.
and with us down under the earth,
it will, in the form of a star,
560.   shine upon our green grave
at dark blue nights.

europe is quiet, once again quiet,
its revolutions are over. . .
shame on it! it has settled down and
565.   its liberty it has not achieved.
they left him alone, completely alone,
the cowardly peoples the magyar;
chains rattle on every hand, only in the
magyar's hand rings the sword.
570.   but must we fall in despair?
must we be sad on this account?
on the contrary, oh nation, rather
let this be what gives us strength.
let this lift our souls,
575.   that we are the candlelight
which, while the rest are aslumber,

is burning in the night of darkness.
if our light were not blazing
through the boundless night,
580.   they might think up there in heaven
that the world has passed away.
glance at us, glance, liberty,
recognize your people now,
while others refuse to shed even tears for you,
585.   we are offering our blood.
or do you need more, so that your blessing
will not be given us undeserved?
in this unfaithful age we you last,
your only believers remain.

BIBLIOGRAPHY

Arany, László. 1898. *Hangsúly és ritmus.* Budapest.

Balassa, József. 1890. Hangsúly a magyar nyelvben. *Nyelvtudományi Közlemények* 21:401-434.

————. 1904. *Magyar fonetika.* Budapest.

Bánhidi, Zoltán, Jókay, Z. and Szabó, D. 1965. *Learn Hungarian.* Second edition. Budapest.

Bárczi, Géza. 1960. *Fonetika.* Budapest.

————. 1963. *A magyar nyelv életrajza.* Budapest.

Brink, B. Ten. 1901. *The language and metre of Chaucer.* London.

Chatman, Seymour. 1957. Linguistics, poetics, and interpretation: the phonemic dimension. *Quarterly Journal of Speech* 43:239-256.

————. 1965. *A theory of meter.* The Hague.

Chomsky, Noam. 1965. *Aspects of the theory of syntax.* Cambridge.

Chomsky, Noam and Halle, Morris. 1968. *The sound pattern of English.* New York.

Classe, Andre. 1939. *The rhythm of English prose.* Oxford.

Collinder, Björn. 1937. Über quantität und intensität. *Neuphilologische Mitteilungen* 38:97-120.

————. 1965. *An introduction to the Uralic languages.* Berkeley.

DuBois, Elizabeth H. 1906. *The stress accent in Latin poetry.* New York.

Fónagy, Iván. 1958. A hangsúlyról. *Nyelvtudományi Értekezések* 18. Budapest.

_____. 1959. *A költöi nyelv hangtanából.* Budapest.

Gábor, Ignác. 1952. *A magyar ritmika válaszútja.* Budapest.

Gáldi, László. 1955. Vers és nyelv. In *Nyelvünk a reformkorban,* ed. D. Pais. Budapest.

_____. 1961. *Ismerjük meg a versformákat.* Budapest.

Gombócz, Zoltán. 1904. Balassa: Magyar Fonetika c. könyvének birálata. *Nyelvtudományi Közlemények* 34: 235-240.

_____. no date. *Összegyüjtött müvei.* Vol. II, ed. G. Laziczius and D. Pais. Budapest.

G. Varga, Györgyi. 1968. *Alakváltozatok a budapesti köznyelvben.* Budapest.

Hall, Robert A. 1944. *Hungarian grammar.* Linguistic Society of America Language Monograph 21. Baltimore.

_____. 1964. *Introductory linguistics.* New York.

Halle, Morris and Keyser, S. J. 1966. Chaucer and the study of prosody. *College English* 28: 187-219.

Hegedűs, Lajos. 1934. *A magyar nemzeti versritmus kérdése.* Pécs.

_____. 1959. *A költöi mesterség: bevezetés a magyar verstanba.* Budapest.

Hill, Archibald A. 1966. English metrics: a restatement. In *Essays in literary analysis.* Austin.

Horváth, János. 1948. *A magyar vers.* Budapest.

_____. 1951. *Rendszeres magyar verstan.* Budapest.

————. 1955. Vitás verstani kérdések. *Nyelvtudományi Értekezések* 7. Budapest.

Jakobson, Roman. 1960. Linguistics and poetics. In *Style in language*, ed. T. A. Sebeok. New York.

Jakobson, Roman and Halle, Morris. 1956. *Fundamentals of language*. Mouton.

Jespersen, Otto. 1900. Notes on metre. *Linguistica*. Reprinted, 1967, in *Essays on the language of literature*, ed. S. Chatman and S. Levin. Boston.

Juhasz, Francis S. 1961. Constructive features in Hungarian. M.A. thesis, Columbia University.

Kecskés, András. 1966. A komplex ritmuselemzés elvi kérdései. *Irodalomtudományi Közlemények* 1-2. Budapest.

Keyser, S. Jay. 1967. The linguistic basis of English prosody. In *Modern studies in English*, ed. D. A. Reibel and S. A. Schane. Englewood Cliffs.

Klemm, Antal. 1942. *Magyar történeti mondattan*. Budapest.

Krámský, Jiři. 1966. On the phonological law of incompatibility of free quantity and free stress. In *Travaux linguistiques de Prague*, ed. J. Vachek. University, Alabama.

László, Zsigmond. 1961. *Ritmus és dallam: a magyar vers és ének prozódiája*. Budapest.

Laziczius, Gyula. 1944. *Fonétika*. Budapest.

Lehiste, Ilse. 1970. Quantity in Estonian language and poetry. To appear in *Essays in Estonian poetry*, ed. A. Raunit. New Haven.

Lehmann, W. P. 1956. *The development of Germanic verse form*. Austin.

Lenneberg, Eric H. 1967. *Biological foundations of language*. New York.

Levin, Samuel. 1964. Poetry and grammaticalness. Proceedings of the Ninth International Congress of Linguists. Reprinted, 1967, in *Essays on the language of literature*, ed. S. Chatman and S. Levin. Boston.

Levý, Jiři. 1969. Mathematical aspects of the theory of verse. In *Statistics and style,* ed. R. Bailey. New York.

Lieberman, Philip. 1967. *Intonation, perception, and language.* Massachusetts Institute of Technology Research Monograph 38. Cambridge.

Lotz, John. no date. *Metrics and linguistics.* Mimeographed.

_____. 1939. *Das ungarische sprachsystem.* Stockholm.

_____. 1942. Notes on structural analysis in metrics. *Helicon* 4:119-146.

_____. 1952. *Hungarian meter.* Stockholm.

_____. 1960. Metric typology. In *Style in language,* ed. T. A. Sebeok. Cambridge.

_____. 1967. Magyar nyelvészeti kutatások az Amerikai Egyesült Államokban. In *A Magyar Nyelv Története és Rendszere,* ed. S. Imre and I. Szathmári. Budapest.

Négyesi, László. 1892. *A mértékes magyar verselés története.* Budapest.

Németh, László. 1940. *Magyar ritmus.* Budapest.

_____. 1963. *A kisérletező ember.* Budapest.

Ohmann, Richard M. 1964. Generative grammars and the concept of literary style. *Word* 20:423-439.

_____. 1966. Literature as sentences. *College English* 27.4:261-267.

Petőfi, Sándor. 1960. *Összes költeményei.* Budapest.

Rákos, Petr. 1966. *Rhythm and metre in Hungarian verse.* Acta Universitatis Carolinae Philologica Monographia XI. Praha.

Rice, Lester A. 1965. Some rules of Hungarian vocalization. M.A. thesis, Indiana University.

————. 1967. Hungarian morphological irregularities with contributions to feature theory. Ph.D. dissertation, Indiana University.

Saporta, Sol. 1960. The application of linguistics to the study of poetic language. In *Style in language,* ed. T. A. Sebeok. Cambridge.

Sauvageot, Aurelien. 1951. *Esquisse de la langue hongroise.* Paris.

Sebeok, Thomas A. 1943. Notes on Hungarian vowel phonemes. *Language* 19:162-164.

Stankiewicz, Edward. 1960. Linguistics and the study of poetic language. In *Style in Language,* ed. T. A. Sebeok. Cambridge.

Sturtevant, E. H. 1940. *The pronunciation of Greek and Latin.* Philadelphia.

Szabédi, László. 1955. *A magyar ritmus formái.* Bukarest-Budapest.

Szathmáry, István, ed. 1961. *A magyar stilisztika útja.* Budapest.

Szépe, György. 1967. A magyar generativ fonológia néhány kérdése. In *A magyar nyelv története és rendszere,* ed. S. Imre and I. Szathmári.

Szinnyei, József. 1912. *Ungarische sprachlehre.* Leipzig.

Tezla, Albert. 1964. *An introductory bibliography to the study of Hungarian literature.* Cambridge.

Thorne, J. P. 1965. Stylistics and generative grammars. *Journal of Linguistics* 1:49-59.

Tompa, József, ed. 1961. *A mai magyar nyelv rendszere.* Vol. I. Budapest.

————, ed. 1962. *A mai magyar nyelv rendszere.* Vol. II. Budapest.

Vargyas, Lajos. 1952. *A magyar nyelv ritmusa.* Budapest.

————. 1966. *Magyar vers—magyar nyelv.* Budapest.

Whitehall, H. and Hill, A. A. 1964. A report on the language-literature seminar. In *Readings in applied English linguistics,* ed. H. B. Allen. Second edition. New York.

Wimsatt, W. K. and Beardsley, M. C. 1959. The concept of meter: an exercise in abstraction. *PMLA* 74:585-598.

Zirmunskij, V. 1966. *Introduction to metrics: the theory of verse.* The Hague.